HATED NIGHTFALL

WOUNDS TO THE FACE

By the same author

Stage Plays
  Stripwell
  Claw
  The Love of a Good Man
  Fair Slaughter
  That Good Between Us
  The Hang of the Gaol
  The Loud Boy's Life
  Birth on a Hard Shoulder
  Crimes in Hot Countries
  The Power of the Dog
  A Passion in Six Days
  Downchild
  Women Beware Women
    (with Thomas Middleton)
  The Possibilities
  The Last Supper
  The Bite of the Night
  Seven Lears
  Golgo
  The Europeans
  Judith
  A Hard Heart
  Hated Nightfall
  Ego in Arcadia
  Wounds to the Face
  Collected Plays Vol. 1
    (Claw, No End of Blame,
    Victory, The Castle,
    Scenes from an Execution)
  Collected Plays Vol. 2
    (The Love of a Good Man,
    The Possibilities, Brutopia,
    Rome, Uncle Vanya, Ten Dilemmas)

TV Plays
  Pity in History
  Brutopia

Radio Plays
  One Afternoon on the 63rd Level of the
    North Face of the Pyramid of
    Cheops the Great
  Henry V in Two Parts
  Herman with Millie and Mick
  Scenes from an Execution
  The Early Hours of a Reviled Man

Poetry
  Don't Exaggerate; Desire and Abuse
  The Breath of the Crowd
  Gary the Thief/Gary Upright
  Lullabies for the Impatient
  Ascent of Monte Grappa

Films
  The Blow
  The Castle

Marionettes
  All He Fears

Opera
  Terrible Mouth

Essays
  Arguments for a Theatre

PLAYSCRIPT 120

HATED NIGHTFALL

WOUNDS TO THE FACE

Howard Barker

CALDER PUBLICATIONS · RIVERRUN PRESS
London · Montreuil · New York

First published in Great Britain in 1994 by
Calder Publications Ltd
9–15 Neal Street, London WC2H 9TU

and in the United States of America in 1994 by
Riverrun Press Inc
1170 Broadway, New York, NY 10001

All performing rights in these plays are strictly reserved and no performance may be given unless a licence has been obtained prior to rehearsal. Applications for a licence should be made to:

Judy Daish Associates Ltd., 83 Eastbourne Mews, London W2 6LQ

The right of Howard Barker to be identified as author of this work has been asserted by him in accordance with the Copyright Design and Patents Act 1988.

British Library Cataloguing-in-Publication Data
Barker, Howard
    Hated Nightfall AND Wounds to the Face.
    (Playscript Series; No. 120)
    I. Title II. Barker, Howard. Wounds to
    the Face. III. Series
    822.914

ISBN 0–7145–4270–9

Library of Congress Cataloging-in-Publication Data
A catalog record of this book is available from the Library of Congress

Typeset in 9/10 pt Times by Pure Tech Corporation, Pondicherry, India
Printed in Great Britain by Hillman Printers (Frome) Ltd, Frome, Somerset

CONTENTS

HATED NIGHTFALL   1

WOUNDS TO THE FACE   51

To
All That Was Not Reconcilled

HATED NIGHTFALL

The Tutor
of
The Romanoffs

His
Exemplification
of
Desire
and Subsequent
Martyrdom
in the
Schoolroom
at
Ekaterinburg
16th July, 1918

Seventy years after the murder of the Russian Imperial family by Revolutionaries, their remains were discovered. Alongside them lay two as yet unidentified human beings.

CHARACTERS

DANCER	A Tutor
ROMANOFF	An Emperor
CAROLINE	An Empress
CHRISTOPHE ⎫	
HELEN ⎬	Their Children
GRISELDA ⎭	
JANE	A Servant
FITCH ⎫	
ARRANT ⎪	
DISBANNER ⎬	Officials of the Revolution
DENADIR ⎪	
ALBEIT ⎭	
A CHORUS	
(To include the above)	

PART ONE

A substantial interior space, barren. A single upright chair on which a
WOMAN *sits asleep. It is the sleep of exhaustion, manifested in her*
posture. The silence is ruptured by the intrusion of orchestral music,
which ceases. In the restored silence, a CHILD *passes, dragging a pillow.*
A MAN *enters. He goes to the sleeping* WOMAN *and places his hands*
kindly on her shoulders.

ROMANOFF: I'm sorry
          I'm sorry
          I'm so sorry
          So sorry
          So sorry (*The* WOMAN *is not awakened. He goes out. A*
SECOND MAN *enters. He stares at the* WOMAN.)
DANCER (*pause*): This will not be my decision the decision comes from
elsewhere rather far away by telephone no not by telephone (*Pause*)
          By telegram and this decision is irrevocable so please don't
entertain hopes of reprieve no messenger will arrive no stained rider on
a lathering horse etcetera no and further more I am the one who (*Pause*)
          I volunteered (*Pause*)
          No one persuaded me or appealed to higher principles (*Pause*)
          I think with a rifle (*Pause*)
          No a knife (*Pause*)
          A rifle or a knife (*Pause*)
          I have a knife whereas a rifle I should need to borrow so what
I can borrow it (*Pause*)
          It is perhaps important the executioner regards himself as a
professional his actions unimpaired by enthusiasm or reluctance in this
case however (*Pause*)
          I confess to very real desire I am immensely (*Pause*)
          Drawn to the task (*Pause*)
          My only fear believe me being that another might offer his
services and the thing degenerate into a competition short and long
straws the tossing of a coin etcetera no when the decision is announced
over the telephone it will be I and no other I alone who (*Pause*)
          Or telegraph I think however the existence of the order its
material existence (*Pause*)
          Incriminating bits of paper (*Pause*)
          Caroline (*Pause*)

Most likely therefore to be the telephone by which (*He stops, aware he is being observed by a* WOMAN *holding a broom and bucket. Pause.*)

JANE: Let her sleep.

DANCER: I'm not stopping her.

JANE (*cleaning the floor*): You're pestering her.

DANCER: Not in the least.

JANE: Muttering and so on.

DANCER: Be quiet you are a servant.

JANE: I am a servant and so are you.

DANCER: A servant and no one cares for your opinions.

JANE: No one cares for them but they still exist.

DANCER: Let them exist but unarticulated.

JANE: Shut up.

DANCER: You shut up.

JANE: No.

DANCER: Do as you are told.

JANE: Of course I won't.

DANCER: Look, her knees have drifted open with that abolition of all consciousness that comes with sleep and if I — (*He cranes.*)

Stoop or — (*and kneels.*)

Kneel —

The shadows fall between her thighs and —

What's there

What's there (*He squirms.* JANE *looks at him. He gets up, brushes his knees.*)

No one will ever understand my attitude to women. Never. (JANE *goes out.*)

So what.

I am never to be understood.

So what.

Let them bury me beneath a tree

An insubstantial tree

Never mind the oaks the urns the obelisks

And when the tree blows down

So what

So what (*He covers his face with his hands. The overture is revived, clamorous. The* CHILD *passes with a pillow.* ROMANOFF *appears. Silence.*)

ROMANOFF: If we are guilty of anything it is an excess of love.

DANCER (*recovering*): Excellent!

Preposterous!

And excellent!

I do so love the apologia of kings!

Hilarity!

Impertinence.

Presumption.

I'm not conducting the trial, someone else is.

ROMANOFF: Love of one another. Consuming love which blinded me to circumstances beyond the wall.

DANCER: Wall? What wall?

ROMANOFF: The wall of love.

DANCER: Is love a wall, then?

ROMANOFF: A wall behind which the most tender flowers of affection, intimacy and —

DANCER: Push her knees together, you are her husband. (*Pause.*
ROMANOFF *glares at him.*)

Her knees. (*Pause*)

Have come apart. (*Pause*)

A wall, is it? I am wholly ignorant of love but that is possibly only a reflection of my dissidence, a characteristic of my revolutionary nature which cannot subscribe to platitudes. Perhaps I know more about love even than you, but love of a different kind. Perhaps at this stage I am obliged to be strictly theoretical about this love, but with the changing circumstances of our time, I might —

ROMANOFF *seizes* DANCER *by the throat. Comic music accompanies his attempt to throttle him. They move to an fro in a terrible embrace. A* CHORUS *of shadowy figures laughs as an accompaniment. The music stops, and the* CHORUS *is silent. Only* DANCER's *laugh is heard, as he adjusts his collar.* ROMANOFF, *exhausted, hangs his head. The* CHILD *is discovered, watching, holding his pillow by its corner.* DANCER *goes to the* CHILD.

DANCER: Your father cannot forgive me, cannot, no matter how he tries, and he is Christian, he is devout! (*He looks at* ROMANOFF.) As to whether I am able to forgive him, that hardly enters into it —

ROMANOFF: Forgive for what?

DANCER: No, no —

ROMANOFF: For what?

DANCER: You see, he cannot even conceive of his offence —

ROMANOFF: For what, I said —

DANCER: What am I, after all, a tutor, a servant, a domestic animal —

ROMANOFF: Please —

DANCER: Which whilst possessing the propensity for craven gratitude —

ROMANOFF: Stop this —

DANCER: Is incapable of registering resentment —

ROMANOFF: Stop, I beg you —

DANCER: **Hatred or contempt** (*The* CHILD *shudders.* DANCER *holds him tight.*) It's all right, it's all right, don't be frightened, what does it matter, after all, I am a transient phenomenon whose own extinction is already written in the Book of Circumstance, yes, a transient phenomenon, can you say that? (*The* CHILD *opens his mouth.*) Yes, quite so, that's what I am, remember that and the firing squad, that also is, look boldly in the barrels of the guns, transient phenomenon, shout . . .! (*He pushes the* CHILD *violently towards* ROMANOFF.)

CHORUS: **Dancer**
Dancer
We think it possible you are a fraud
DANCER: I never rule it out, gentlemen!
CHORUS: **And we will pay a price to follow you**
DANCER: Yes, why shouldn't you? Pay the price and be damned!
CHORUS: **Dancer**
What kind of tutor were you?
DANCER: Not nice, obviously.
CHORUS: **All your certificates were forged**
DANCER: Yes, I am without qualifications! On the other hand, I am blessed with this extraordinary facility for speech. Words tumble. Words froth. And in the proper order! Now, stop pestering me, I am expecting a communication of the highest significance. (*He turns.*)
CHORUS: **Dancer**
DANCER: What!
CHORUS: **If you were a liar under one regime**
How can we tell
You will not lie under another? (*Pause.* DANCER *is patient.*)
DANCER: Listen, the words are moribund. The words are wasted with disease. They haunt old libraries as sick men creep the corridors of sanitoria. (*He smiles.*)
New words, please . . . (*He goes to leave, turns swiftly.*)
You want me to confess!
Confession is your solitary need. (*Pause*)
I do not confess. The instinct is missing in me . . . (*He looks at them, provocatively.*)
I leapt into the fireplace as a baby, from my mother's arms, which is why I have this scar on me. Why, I wonder? Did I think no flame could scorch me? (*Pause*)
I'll perish, obviously, and in a ghastly way. Take comfort from the fact that I shall suffer. The world abhors me. It writhes to know I walk upon its surfaces . . . (*He is suddenly possessed.*)
I jump on it (*He jumps, stops, laughs.*)
Oh, the pathos of the man who cannot assent, for assent he must . . . eventually . . . (*The* CHORUS *turns to leave.*)
Stay with me . . .!
Oh, stay . . .!
CHORUS: **Dancer**
Circumstances elevate unlikely men
The wave that lifted you
Will swallow you again (*They leave.* DANCER *turns.*)
DANCER: Thirty years a tutor! And I was handsome, yes, I had the looks, I had the acumen, and so many learned from me, what could I not teach? For example
The ambiguities of parental love
I saw it all
The tortures of domestic bliss

I've seen the instruments
Oh, the terrible ordeal of infants
Especially the rich
Pity the rich
I do (*He turns to* ROMANOFF.)

I am best qualified to govern you, believe me, I have your interests at heart. (*He sits, dismissing* ROMANOFF *with a slight gesture.*) Go now, but leave your wife. (ROMANOFF *takes his son by the shoulder.*) How appallingly she sleeps. Disaster she interprets as a sickness, which can be healed by diet or a period of rest . . .

ROMANOFF: She is depressed.

DANCER: Yes.

ROMANOFF: She deserved nothing but love.

DANCER: Mm.

ROMANOFF: Gratitude.

DANCER: Mm.

ROMANOFF: And loyalty.

DANCER: Indeed.

ROMANOFF: A perfect mother. A perfect wife.

DANCER: Why are you rehearsing this?

ROMANOFF: **Because our misery is incomprehensible to me**. (*Pause. He shrugs.*) Not entirely. I am the guilty one. And I have brought these innocents to the brink of murder. (*Pause. He turns to go.*) Don't kill my son. (*Pause*)

DANCER: Why not? (*A slow, pitiful shrug arises from* ROMANOFF's *shoulders. He leads the* CHILD *away.*)
Innocents? (DANCER *gets up.*)
Innocents?
Thank God I am not young, oh, the words of the young, the ponderous vocabulary of youth, their phrases dip like over-laden freighters, morality and rectitude strapped to the decks
Innocent of what? (*A wind whispers round the room.* DANCER *looks at the sleeping* WOMAN.)
I am innocent if anybody is . . . (*Two young* WOMEN *appear, pensive, anxious, they wait for his attention. He detects them, looks up.*)

HELEN: Are you in charge now, Citizen?

DANCER: Me, yes.

HELEN: Ridiculous!

DANCER: Isn't it?

HELEN: Only a week ago we were studying the Gallic Wars. The tribes. The topography.

DANCER: So we were . . .

HELEN: It's all so incomprehensible to us . . .

DANCER: Is it? So your father says. And yet it is so lucid to me.

GRISELDA: And I hate calling people Citizen!

DANCER: Do you? Say it more often, and it will cease to offend you.

HELEN: What we find particularly hard to understand is why —

DANCER: Please, do not inflict me with the poverty of your understanding.
I am no longer a teacher. Your ignorance is no longer a concern of mine.
(GRISELDA *weeps. Her* SISTER *clasps her.*) Oh, how I long to make
you weep . . . how gratifying the spectacle of a young girl's tears!

HELEN: You are vile and —

DANCER: **All things cowardly and reprehensible I know**. (*Pause. He
smiles.*)
And once you trusted me.

HELEN: No. Not entirely.

DANCER: Yes.

HELEN: Not entirely, I said —

DANCER: **You trusted me**. (*Pause*)
Why pretend to insights you could not possibly possess? None
of you has the slightest subtlety of mind —

HELEN: That isn't true!

DANCER: Helen, I know your mediocrity . . . (*She turns away, bitterly.*)
You trusted me, and now you are ashamed. You are ashamed of your
own disingenuousness . . . (*He shrugs.*) What does it matter? We are all
dead now . . .

HELEN: I hate you Citizen . . .

DANCER: Very well, I am hated . . . and yet the sun still shines . . .

HELEN (*turning on him*): **It is dead matter, that is why. Volatile, but
lifeless** . . . (*He stares at her.*) Shall we be killed?

DANCER: I think so, yes.

HELEN: Save my little sister —

DANCER: She is not little, she has merely failed to mature —

HELEN: Oh, stop this fatuous and futile —

DANCER (*rising to his feet*): **I can't help it, I can't help it . . .!** (*He
pushes them.*) Get outside, now, get outside, find a corner and wait to be
killed . . .! (*They stare. He shudders. Pause.*) I am fifty. My chance has
come. **Fifty and absolute**. (*Pause*)

GRISELDA: You are not really bad, Citizen . . .

DANCER: I am —

GRISELDA: No, not really, really bad —

DANCER: I am
I am that bad (*Pause*)
Believe me.
You merely cannot bear to contemplate it. (*He touches* GRI-
SELDA *weakly on the shoulder.*)
Go away now. I am capable of such artificial sentiments,
things that make my own flesh crawl . . . (*Suddenly* GRISELDA *seizes
his hand and kisses it. He withdraws it.*)
You see . . .! You see how colonized we are by other people's
gestures! On the rim of the grave even you are insincere! Too many
novels, Miss! Too many plays! (GRISELDA *bursts into tears and
hurries out.* HELEN *boldly keeps her ground.*)

HELEN: I pity you, Citizen.

DANCER: Oh, don't bother . . .!

HELEN: Pity, I said —

DANCER: **I mock your pity. I repudiate your pity. Take your pity to death's ditch with you**. (HELEN *stares in disbelief, then goes out. He watches her departure. A* MAN *has entered, with a sheaf of papers. He looks at* DANCER, *bemused*.)

FITCH: You'll hurt yourself.

DANCER: Hurt myself? How?

FITCH: All this effort to be vile.

DANCER: No effort, I assure you.

FITCH: It's not required. (DANCER *turns to him at last*.)

No one suspects you of disloyalty.

DANCER: Don't they? I suspect myself of it.

FITCH: Well, that is consistent with the earnestness with which you have adopted the revolutionary cause, Citizen, and wholly laudable, but —

DANCER: I do hate that (*Pause*)

Forgive me

I do hate that — confectionery — of words I tell you a truth and you offer me these impeccably

I am talking for example of

These immaculately

My sexuality

Its lethal nature

Coiffured words

We must be careful, mustn't we, not to smother things in words?

This woman has not woken yet

No, that helps nobody. (*Pause.* FITCH *stares at him*.)

FITCH: I have to go . . .

DANCER: What are these papers? I receive so many papers and quite frankly they are not always read . . . (*Pause*)

Their appearance is detrimental . . .

And what are they? The usual exhortations to solidarity . . . quotations from the works of dead economists and completely biased news, no one places the slightest credence in them, you would need to be the most diseased fanatic to even (*He stops*.)

FITCH: Please, put your criticisms on paper and I will forward them to the appropriate committee.

DANCER: Yes, I will. (FITCH *turn to go.* DANCER *hurries to him and stabs him.* FITCH *cries out in disbelief*.)

Oh . . .!

Oh . . .! (*The* CHORUS *appears, with* JANE. *A frantic, anxious cascade of music*.)

You see, if they don't listen to me, what occurs!

CHORUS: **Dancer**

We can forgive the revolutionary death but this

DANCER: I've killed!

CHORUS: **This**

DANCER: It's easy! I'm amazed!

CHORUS: **This**

JANE: He isn't dead . . .

DANCER: I've killed, I said!

CHORUS: **The tutor is a murderer**

DANCER (*turning on them*): **The educator always is**. (*Pause*. FITCH *stirs on the ground*.)

JANE: Not dead I said. (*Pause. Silence but for a thin wind blowing*.)

DANCER: I'll try again.

JANE: You'll have to. (*Pause*. FITCH *moans*. DANCER *offers* JANE *the knife*.)

DANCER: You do it. (*The* CHORUS *laughs*.)

       Why shouldn't she? (*Pause*. JANE *has not taken the knife*.)

       All right . . . I will . . . (*He goes to* FITCH, *who sees him*.)

FITCH: I'm hurt . . .

DANCER: Yes, you are . . . so badly hurt you can't come back . . . it's . . . a matter of — (*He hacks the throat brutally, his eyes shut*.)

CHORUS: **Dancer**

       Dancer

       You are insane

DANCER (*swiftly rising to his feet*): You would say that! How necessary you should think I am insane! Think so if it relieves you! (*With a gesture of contempt he tosses the knife away*.)

JANE: He's still not dead . . .

DANCER (*turning on her now*): **If you know so much about it, do it**. (*She is adamantly still*.)

       He is in pain there, and really, I am an amateur . . . (*She stares*.)

       Haven't you killed cattle, sheep and things? (*Pause*)

       So what if he's in pain. He was an idiot. (*To* CHORUS.)

       That is an authentic idiot,

       Not me . . .

CHORUS: **Dancer**

       You have stabbed the agent of the Revolution

       He was on your side!

DANCER: *My* side?

       Do I have a side? (*They are aghast*.)

       Oh, how horrified you are to find me pure . . .

       Yes . . .

       Rinsed of all belief . . .

       You'd prefer any old catechism to the echo of the unbeliever

       Lies

       Filth

       Encrusted ideology

DANCER *walks coolly to the dying* MAN *and slits his throat, this time effectively and in a routine manner. As he moves away he senses he is watched and turns to see* CHRISTOPHE, *in a corner of the stage. The* CHILD *tilts his toy watering-can. A dark fluid trickles out . . .* DANCER *turns back to the* CHORUS.

DANCER: Humans really are enslaved by books

I'll give you a book

Oh, I intend to write one

I am as narcissistic as the next man (*He wipes the blade of the knife this time and pockets it.*)

I say a book

I must warn you, I mean a shelf (*He laughs.*)

Yes!

And you will memorize it, oh, whole paragraphs word-perfectly . . . (*He looks at the* CHORUS. *They drift away.* JANE *looks at* DANCER.)

Swab away the blood.

JANE: Swab it yourself.

DANCER: Jane, you are a servant

JANE: I am a servant, and so are you.

DANCER: Must we go through this every hour? I tell you for the first and last time, I am a law unto myself.

JANE: You're Billy the tutor with the balding bonce as far as I'm concerned.

DANCER: Oh, your rustic charm . . .! Swab it, I said.

JANE: No. (*Pause. He takes the bucket and broom away from her and begins to wash the floor.*)

DANCER: 'Make my criticisms on paper and forward them to the Committee . . .!' What does he think I am, a suicide?

JANE: He asked for it.

DANCER: I'm nobody's fool.

JANE: That's true, Citizen. But perhaps it's no bad thing to be a fool . . .?

DANCER (*stopping, appearing to think*): The ramifications of such an opinion stretch even my imagination to breaking point . . . (*He lays down the broom, goes to move the body.*) I so detest the wisdom of the people . . . you take this arm.

JANE: Nope.

DANCER: Oh, come on . . .

JANE: No I said. (*Pause.* DANCER *tries to drag the body by its arms. It scarcely moves.*)

DANCER: The bulk of humanity suspends its entire existence from three or four bucolic and inane proverbs. This enables it to — (*He heaves.*) tolerate its own annihilation, even . . . (*He drops the arms and goes to the legs, and pulls.*) Jane . . . (*She ignores him. He pulls again.*) The lyrics of some whimpering ballad can compensate them for the most appalling blows of fate **I can't move this by myself**. (*She watches, still.*)

You will remember this moment. My apparent helplessness. My apparent foolishness. You will recollect it. The nadir, possibly, of my existence. I hope you will not rue the day . . .

JANE *goes out.* DANCER *is still for a long time. A light, pastoral music, he stares at the sleeping* WOMAN. *He goes to her, and leaning close to her ear, whispers. He looks to assure himself he is alone, then proceeds to whisper in her other ear. He tears himself away in a paroxysm of ecstasy.*

DANCER: I wonder
              I wonder if
              This
              Passion
              Is
              Sincere
              The distinction between an honest and dishonest passion being
                                                              what precisely

              Well
              I essay
              I tentatively
              And
              Humbly
              Propose (*He laughs, shaking his head.*)
              Typical tutor
              Typical philosophe
              Nothing is experienced but needs to be explained! (*He reflects.
He makes an effort to achieve perfect expression.)
              Princesses sleep a thousand years and Queens perish on the
                                                              block

              We so adore
              We so adore to (*He whispers torrentially into the* WOMAN's
ear, and turns away abruptly.)
              And I am after all a modern man
              Yes
              Nothing quaint or archaic clings to me
              They also require me to die
              Humiliation
              Is
              Their
              Apotheosis . . . (*He looks at her, half-pityingly.* ROMANOFF
enters. DANCER *senses him.*)
              I am pitying her death . . .
ROMANOFF: And what of yours?
DANCER: Mine?

              I expect it hourly, and from any source but don't come near me
I have a knife which I have just employed in an almost but not quite
arbitrary manner
              There is the man of the future throat cut
              Typical future
              Short-lived and banal
              Promises and inexorable laws of
              Engineer of human souls etcetera
              Dead now
              Never mind
              So keep your distance
              Would you kindly help me move him I was rather too sponta-
neous and he fell right in the door

Next time

Plan it better obviously (*Pause.* ROMANOFF *shakes his head.*)

What are you, a saint? (ROMANOFF *looks away.*)

Some say you are but I keep an open mind

Drag the corpse away or I will do some cruel thing to those you love. (ROMANOFF *thinks briefly.*)

ROMANOFF: Drag him where?

DANCER: Anywhere, you choose. (ROMANOFF *goes to the dead man, looks.*) I fear my own death for one reason only, that it would render me incapable of experiencing the particular act of love I know myself to be supremely capable of . . .

ROMANOFF: You . . .?

DANCER: Yes. (ROMANOFF *studiedly declines to reply. He leans to the corpse. His hand falters.*)

ROMANOFF: I have never touched a dead man . . .

DANCER: This act of love may not at first be recognizable as such. I think it will be misrepresented. The subtlest minds may be required to identify and elaborate it. (*Pause*)

ROMANOFF: **And that is why we failed** . . .!

DANCER: Please, you are forever analyzing this thing you call your failure, who cares about your failure, already it is of negligible importance, the preposterous fantasy of academics, and nostalgic picture books —

ROMANOFF: **The prince must touch** . . . (*Pause*)

DANCER: Yes . . . (*He shrugs.*)

But the princess, what of her . . .? (ROMANOFF *stands away.*)

ROMANOFF: I decline to do your dirty work for you! Punish as you will. But spare my children —

DANCER: Shhh —

ROMANOFF: Inflict your malice where you will but —

DANCER: Please, you are so — extreme, indulgent —

ROMANOFF: **Me**?

DANCER: You, yes — indulgent with your fear —

ROMANOFF: **You threatened me**.

DANCER: Did I? I forget . . . (*He shrugs.*) I threaten everybody . . . (*He gets up.*)

Come on, help me conceal him or I shall be discovered and consequently you will find yourself in the hands of someone for whom no ties of sentiment restrain his violence . . . (*He smiles.*)

Oh, believe me, I entertain obscure feelings of devotion for you all! Yes! Now, take his legs! (ROMANOFF *hesitates, returns to the body, stoops.* DANCER *does not move, but watches, and then laughs.*)

Yes . . . (ROMANOFF *looks up.*)

It is so — (*He selects the word.*)

Necessary —

The Prince should be porter to a lout. (ROMANOFF *is patient.*)

I am the lout. (*He goes to the arms. Together they hoist the corpse.* DANCER *does not move.*)

I am not presumptious, am I? I do not call myself History. The Agent of Destiny. Justice. The People's Will. I don't drape myself.

DANCER *nods his head.* ROMANOFF *staggers. They go out with the body. An effect of sound and light. A cry. The* CHILD *passes dragging its pillow. The cry again. The sleeping* WOMAN *is aroused, shocked from her state. She speaks as if resuming a diatribe suspended by a spell.*

CAROLINE: Logic . . .! The contemptible and threadbare thing how dare you bring it near me its smell offends me! (*Pause. She perceives her situation, looking side to side, almost surreptitiously. A wind rattles.*)
> That's what I'll say. (*Pause*)
> Because a princess cannot possibly negotiate the nature of her privilege. Conceding even, that it could be argued would be a profound mistake **I am not in the same domain of law let alone language**
>> No
>> Royalty has no defence
>> Shoot me
>> Silence is most eloquent and I shan't utter one syllable of expiation
>> I am not culpable
>> **God is the sole judge of all monarchy**
>> They know that
>> They want to drag us through their courts
>> They want to smear us with their language
>> **I want a priest, please!** (*Silence. She is still. She smiles.*)
> I thought I was modern. I read modern books, but one must be careful of these things, keeping abreast of course but not permitting oneself to be
>> **Penetrated**
>> **Spiked**
>> **Some specimen of etymology pinned to the board**
>> Darling, come here! (*The* CHILD *is discovered standing forlornly. She opens her arms.*)
> I was asleep! I do sleep such sleeps, don't I, deeper than cats certainly, more like a toad! They sleep whole winters!
>> Come here! (*The* CHILD *approaches her, slowly. She kneels.*)
>> Who knows why I sleep so? Or what wakes me? (*She bites her lip. She caresses him.*)
> Things are so very out of order . . .! But what is certain is that order reasserts itself.
>> It must
>> That is a law
>> Do you know what a law is?
>> A law is what cannot be disputed
>> So

All this
Inconvenience
Will last for such and such a time
A week perhaps!
But not longer
Promise you
Promise
Promise (*She suddenly crushes him.*)
Little Monarch
How they hate you . . .!
But don't hate them because it would demean you
Their hatred is the proof we are elect! (*She suddenly repulses

him.*)

Quick now, find your sisters! Find Helen! (*He starts to go.*)
Listen . . .! (*He stops.*)

When you are the monarch, remember this! To suffer also
is the privilege of princes! (*The* CHILD *goes out, as* ROMANOFF
returns. She sees his state.)

You are covered in mud!

ROMANOFF: Yes . . .

CAROLINE: Why?

ROMANOFF: Dancer asked me to assist him with a —

CAROLINE: Dancer asked —

ROMANOFF: Not asked exactly —

CAROLINE: Dancer —

ROMANOFF: **Ordered me** —

CAROLINE: **Dancer is a tutor** —

ROMANOFF: **Ordered me I said**. (*Pause*)

CAROLINE: You see, I am awake. (*She shrugs.*)

I wake, and it is arbitrary, just as it is arbitrary when I go to
sleep. Something is preparing me for death. (*She shrugs again.*)

I say death . . . (*She looks at him.*)

The death of something . . . obviously . . .

ROMANOFF: Everything is my fault.

CAROLINE: Yes.

ROMANOFF (*horrified*): Do you believe that, Caroline?

CAROLINE: Yes.

ROMANOFF: And in what may be our final hours you are prepared to
burden me with the entire responsibility for what's —

CAROLINE: Absolutely, yes. (ROMANOFF *looks at her, distraught.
She experiences a surge of pity.*) Oh, come here, little mouse . . .

ROMANOFF (*fixed to the spot*): My son — my innocent and inoffensive
son —

CAROLINE: Come here, I said . . . (ROMANOFF *silently chokes tears.*)
Always we called one another little mouse . . . (ROMANOFF *does not
take her hand. It falters.*)

ROMANOFF: I am without sin. Blameless and without sin.

CAROLINE: Yes.

But I require another life. (ROMANOFF *looks at her, bewildered.*)

The one about to close I . . . do not feel, on reflection, fulfilled my needs . . . (*His mouth hangs open with incredulity. The* DAUGHTERS *enter.*)

HELEN: Mother!

CAROLINE: Shh! (*She gestures them impatiently with a hand. They stop, also puzzled.* CAROLINE *walks.*)

I do not want to die. (*She looks, one to the other.*)

HELEN: We neither! And we are frightened, Mother!

CAROLINE: Yes.

But whereas I think I possess the means of my deliverance, I am not certain either of you do . . . (*Pause. They follow her movements.*)

In my sleeps, I hear voices. These voices urge me to — (*She laughs.*)

Oh, all sorts of things, both poetry and the most obscene —

ROMANOFF: Caroline —

CAROLINE: Preposterous and —

ROMANOFF: Caroline —

CAROLINE (*turning to him*): Degenerate things . . . (*Pause*)

ROMANOFF: These sleeps are sickness, Caroline . . .

CAROLINE: Yes, and like all sickness, they originate in God . . . (*She turns to the* GIRLS.)

I tell you this because — in the most unkind way — oh, such a very unkind way — I never felt a greater distance existed between myself and you . . . (*They look to their* FATHER.)

When you would think, under such circumstances —

ROMANOFF: Christophe, Helen, Griselda —

CAROLINE: A mother would manifest the opposite tendency, if anything, an excess of intimacy —

ROMANOFF: Christophe, Helen, Griselda —

CAROLINE: A tidal wave of all those maternal instincts which impending murder —

ROMANOFF: **Christophe**
 Helen
 Griselda (*He shudders.* CAROLINE *is by contrast, icy.*)

CAROLINE: Licenses . . . (*Pause*)

There is no priest, is there? They killed him in the hospital. (*She laughs.*)

All the buildings are misused . . .! The hospital became a slaughterhouse, and as for the schoolroom . . . (*She gestures to the room they are in.*)

Who knows what we shall learn in here?

HELEN: Frankly Mother, I preferred it when you slept all the time —

ROMANOFF: Helen —

HELEN: I did! When she slept, it was possible to invent her, whereas awake she is —

Not nice, is she? (*She looks boldly at* CAROLINE.)

Not that it matters, if you are being killed, what — (*She falters.*)

Memory is ...! (ROMANOFF *goes to console her. She pulls away from him.*)

No! (CAROLINE *laughs.*)

We are forever — grasping one another — I don't wish to be grasped ...!

ROMANOFF: It is not *grasping* ...

HELEN: It feels like it ...

ROMANOFF: Always we were intimate ... what has happened here? Always we embraced ... and you call it grasping ...

HELEN: It's suffocating ...!

GRISELDA (*suddenly*): Where is Christophe?

ROMANOFF: We kissed, always, and on the mouth, we were not reserved, God knows —

HELEN: That was happiness, kissing from happiness somehow is different from this —

GRISELDA: Christophe isn't here ...!

HELEN: **Perpetual comforting!** I do it myself! (*She turns to* GRISELDA.) Don't I? I am the first!

GRISELDA: Christophe isn't here! (*She turns to go and look for the* CHILD. *As she does so,* DANCER *enters, the* CHILD *on his shoulders. Instinctively, they crowd together.*)

DANCER: **He is not critical**

He is not ethical

He can't discriminate

Where is his guilt, therefore? (*He turns about, amusing the* CHILD.)

He does not arbitrate

He cannot calculate

No one could like him more

Than

Me ... (*Pause*)

Paradox ... (*Pause*)

The executioner's affection for his victim ...

Paradoxical! (*To the* CHILD.) Do you know that word?

No?

I paid too little attention to vocabulary, that's obvious, and far too much to grammar! (*He lifts the* CHILD *off his shoulders.*)

I found him staring at me! There I was, spade in hand, ankle-deep in grave-making, and I sensed these melancholy eyes upon me. At once I ceased my labours, which were in any case, too strenuous for me. I was obliged to find another solution to the trivial problem I had set myself. I am in his debt, I might have put my back out ...

GRISELDA (*extending a hand to the* CHILD, *who has been staring at* DANCER): Christophe ...! (*The* CHILD *does not react.*)

CAROLINE: He hardly speaks now ... it is as if he knew the dynasty concludes with him ... (*A single resonant sound announces the presence of the* CHORUS, *who have entered unobserved.* DANCER *advances on them.*)

DANCER: Patience . . .!

Patience . . .! (*He claps his hands at them, they inch back.*)

CHORUS: **Dancer**
Dancer

DANCER: I promise you nothing will occur without your acquiescence!

CHORUS: **You are a calculating and unfathomable man**

DANCER: And would you have me otherwise? Are our enemies not calculating? Do you want me fathomed by the likes of them? This family is steeped in treachery! (*He shrugs.*)

Sophisticated treachery. Educated treachery.

I am a transient phenomenon, but these . . .!

Four hundred years of . . .! (*He shakes his head. The* CHORUS *goes, warily.*)

They have the curiosity of cattle . . . the comic and yet faintly menacing curiosity of cattle . . .

The piercing sound of a telephone. It transfixes everyone. DANCER *is swaying with anticipation, yet quite unable to move. Apprehension has seized the entire* FAMILY. *At last,* JANE *appears.*

JANE: Are you answering that? (DANCER *cannot find a voice. It rings on, with increasing violence.*)

Are you or not? (DANCER *doesn't speak. It stops.*)

DANCER: Oh . . . (*Pause. His body relaxes.*)

They'll ring back, no doubt. (*It rings again.*)

They have rung back. (*He goes out, slowly. It stops.*)

JANE: I'm in favour. (*Pause*)

HELEN: In favour of what?

JANE: Goodness.

HELEN: Are you? Then tell the world what is happening to us!

JANE: I will do.

ROMANOFF: No, go now!

JANE: I can't go now, I've got so much to do —

HELEN: Please, now!

JANE: I promise, when everything is over, I will tell, I won't miss out a single bit of it —

ROMANOFF: No, that's too late, you must go now and —

CAROLINE: **You are making idiots of yourselves**. (*Pause*)

JANE: If you've jewellery . . . watches or anything . . . (*They are silent. She shrugs.*)

I'm not unkind.

I believe in God.

Also, I believe in monarchy.

I believe in all things that are natural.

Like God.

Like monarchy.

And Mr Dancer, I'm sorry to say, is also natural.

Everything that happens, I will tell.

Honestly. (*She goes out. Pause.*)

HELEN: Is that evil? (*Pause*)

Is that the absolute in evil?

ROMANOFF: If I had a gun, I would kill. I, who have never killed, would kill and kill . . .!

CAROLINE: Shut up . . .

ROMANOFF: A man with such a placid disposition must always look absurd when driven to making threats, but —

CAROLINE: If you had a gun you would not use it —

ROMANOFF: **I would, I would, I would . . .!**

GRISELDA: Please, don't quarrel —

ROMANOFF: During the last offensive of the war it was I who gave the order to advance, I alone accept responsibility, no, **I claim it, I claim the thirty thousand dead!**

CAROLINE: You are hardly placid at all . . .

ROMANOFF: I am not placid, no —

GRISELDA: This is ridiculous!

ROMANOFF: I wish I had another life! I wish! I wish!

DANCER *enters. A fall of silence. He is simultaneously apprehensive and vulgar, arrogant, tender. He walks, feeling their eyes upon him. He gestures, in a Roman manner, to himself . . .*

DANCER: The Doorman of our Century . . . (*A stillness. The wind in the boards.*) Me . . . (*He shakes his head. He laughs. He stops.*)

Great moments of human endeavour stimulate a sort of poetry . . . the mundane minds of lawyers are shaken from the attic to the basements . . .

Earthquakes of phraseology . . . the sudden discovery of

The

Style

Of

Rome (*He laughs, bending, shaking his head.*)

He was — you could feel it through the crackling of the telephone, through snow and hail and regiments of rocket launchers, saboteurs, air raids, you name it, it was conspiring to spoil the moment but he was not thrown, he knew this message called for poise and the ponderous delivery of never-to-be-forgotten syllables, a compromise between electrification and the oratorial manner of the late Republic, Cato, Mirabeau, oh, the competition, but he persevered, and it was excellent in many ways, I don't criticize

Yes

He

Says (*The wind again. He stares.*)

And I, the transient phenomenon, will open the door to a new — (*He shakes his head, wearily, then recovers.*)

> I like the new
> The new what
> The new anything
> The New itself
> **It conceals my transience from me!** (*He looks at them.*)
> And your extermination is the threshold . . . (*He grins.*)

I say extermination because death apparently is inadequate, there has to be **obliteration** or someone, some superstitious, crippled-with-religion, infantile, irrational — you know the sort of idiot — will excavate and find a bone, a glove or something and there will be

> **A cult of monarchy**
> Yes

The Citizen at the far end of the telephone has studied History he reads he spent five years in an English library eyes down too, no looking up for passing skirt or knicker he was pellucid on the subject affirmative and absolute that not a shred of any one of you should persist . . . (*Pause*)

> **A problem in itself** (*Pause*)
> He left that to me, of course
> Mere detail
> Couldn't expect him to
> What with his responsibilities
> I had this staggering compliment
> What more could I
> Might have made him angry
> **The Doorman of the Century** surely knows a thing or two

about (*Pause*)

> Acid, presumably . . . (*Pause.* ROMANOFF *looks at him, shaking his head in disbelief.*)

ROMANOFF: You do not want to do this thing . . . I do not believe you honestly wish to do this thing, Mr Dancer . . .

DANCER: Honestly . . . I wonder if I hear you right . . . did you say honestly . . .?

HELEN: **You know very well he said honestly.**

DANCER (*turning on her*): It's such a quaint word! Such an exotic notion, picturesque, obscure!

ROMANOFF: **Examine yourself and** —

DANCER: Oh, please —

ROMANOFF: **Confront your conscience** —

DANCER: **Examine the labyrinth** . .! Hands and knees . .! Magnifying glass . . .! (CAROLINE *laughs*, ROMANOFF, *losing control, slaps her.*)

> **Stop that**
> **Detestable**
> **Brutality**
> **Stop that**

GRISELDA: Daddy . . .!

CAROLINE: Yes, restrain your father if you can, everything he says is calculated to aggravate the situation —

DANCER: The resort to violence is the very hallmark of domesticity . . . (*He turns away.*)

How I shuddered . . .

Something in this family made me recoil, as if I'd touched a loathsome thing which lay hidden under foliage . . .

HELEN: It is you who is the loathsome thing, and it is you who lay hidden under foliage . . .! (*He looks at her. Pause.*)

DANCER: The toad was once a prince . . . and the prince . . . he bears the character of the toad . . . (*He smiles.*)

Go now, and walk together in the grounds, hand in hand, with that slow pace which always seemed to me not so much a demonstration of assurance, power, continuity, but the restraint of madness . . . a measured defiance of decline . . . (*They look to* ROMANOFF. *He leads them out.*) Take coats . . .! (*They stop.*) You might take cold . . . (*Pause.* ROMANOFF *looks at the floor.*)

ROMANOFF: This is a pleasure to you . . . (*He shakes his head, uncomprehending. They go out.* DANCER *watches, then claps his hands swiftly. The* CHORUS *enter, bearing a large table, covered in immaculate white linen and dressed with vases, candelabra, crockery. They stagger it to the middle of the room, go out, and return with chairs.* DANCER, *in a sort of ecstasy, fusses.*)

DANCER: And all I want is love . . .! (*The* CHORUS *laughs, staccato, in unison.*)

It's true!

I think of nothing else, it is the single and obsessive object of my life! (*And again*)

You laugh! (*And again*)

You laugh because the poverty of your imagination blinds you to the possibility! The circumstances seem to abolish it! I assure you, the most comely children are the product of the most squalid copulations, it's the comedy of nature! (*They laugh.*)

Laugh, it's obligatory! (*They stop. They are suddenly dark.*)

CHORUS: **Dancer**

The circumstances which created you are

DANCER: Shhh!

CHORUS: **The flood which carried you this far will certainly**

DANCER: I am not naive . . .

CHORUS: **Recede**

DANCER: I know it all . . .

CHORUS: **Leaving your body hanging in the trees** . . . (DANCER *shrugs, eloquently.*)

DANCER: What you describe as a rebuke to me, is no more or less than my desire . . . (*He nods as if in gratitude. The* CHORUS *goes out. A* FIGURE *is discovered observing* DANCER. *He wears an overcoat, glasses. There is a quality of authority in him.* DANCER *catches him in the corner of his eye.*)

Citizen Fitch . . .! Have you seen him? He is regular as clockwork, and I must confess, his pile of documents becomes almost an

addiction to me — we rely on such people to deliver, don't we, in all
weathers . . .?

　　　　　Perhaps the terrorists got him. I do hope not. (*The* FIGURE
just looks.)

　　　　　Or are you his substitute? (*And looks.*)

　　　　　People come and go . . .

ARRANT (*going to a seat, and sitting*): They say you are learned,
Citizen . . .

DANCER: Do they? Well, they are correct for once.

ARRANT: Are they not always so?

DANCER: Sometimes their innate correctness is distorted by the falsifi-
cations of perspective induced by crisis. I compare the wisdom of the
people to a figure wandering in a hall of mirrors. Always the individual
recognizes himself, but in grotesque forms. This nightmare of percep-
tions does not preclude the existence of a proper mirror, which, the more
outrageous the reflections, the more certain he becomes in his faith that
it does exist, must exist, and above all, will exist, so long as he does not
give up hope. (*Pause*)

　　　　　Hope is the problem, given that for most of us, it is not a
bottomless well. (*Pause*)

　　　　　I am mixing my metaphors . . .!

　　　　　Mirrors. . . . wells. . . . (*Pause*)

　　　　　Yes, of course I'm learned, what about you? (*Pause*)

ARRANT: Faith . . . (*Pause*)

DANCER: Yes.

ARRANT: In the future . . .

DANCER: Yes.

ARRANT: Our children's children . . .

DANCER: Them especially . . . (*Suddenly*) I don't have any children . . .!
(*Pause. He laughs.*) So what? Other people do . . . (ARRANT *stares at*
DANCER.) You stare a great deal. I've noticed, since the Revolution, a
vast increase in staring. Fitch used to do it! (*Pause*) Still does do it, I
expect . . . are you staying, or . . . I've things to do . . . (*Pause*) This
staring is supposed to wreck the nerves, a sort of permanent interroga-
tion . . . I don't mind it myself . . . (*He laughs.*) Of course I mind it, for
one thing I think it's rude . . . (*Pause*)

ARRANT: Rudeness?

DANCER: Yes, staring and conversations in which one party confines
himself to single words must be construed as rudeness . . . (*Pause*) Under
the old regime . . .! (*He laughs.*)

　　　　　I know all the proper answers, Citizen! (*He walks boldly to
the table, adjusts a glass or two.*)

ARRANT: Let's talk about faith . . .

DANCER: Faith? Any time! But you begin. After all, you initiated this
discussion and I haven't the least idea who you are nor whether you
possess the authority to be here, whether you are a charlatan, a counter-
revolutionary or simply a man who has stolen a decent overcoat and
wandered off the street . . .! Things are like that now, it is a paradise for

imposters, but I don't criticize, I take you at face value, and if you are an imposter, so what, the people have the right to engage their masters in discussion at a moment's notice!

> I agree with it! (*He grins.*)
>
> I said masters! You flinched! (*He laughs.*)
>
> Do take your coat off. (ARRANT *looks.*)
>
> There you go! Staring again! At least undo the neck. (*Pause*)
> Citizen. (*Long pause. A wind blows.*)

ARRANT: What distinguishes the rebel from the revolutionary is faith.

DANCER: Yes . . .

ARRANT: The rebel has none.

DANCER: He has no point of reference but himself.

ARRANT: Consequently he cannot be relied upon.

DANCER: Not relied upon, no. But used, perhaps?

> How can you sit buttoned up like that? This room is swelter-
ing. Are you about to leave?

ARRANT: I discomfort you, Citizen.

DANCER (*shrugging*): I am discomforted by the spectacle of a man with too much clothing on.

ARRANT: Or too little?

DANCER: That also would offend me! I think it must be the remnants of some decadent belief in hospitality. The taking of coats, and so on, a servile instinct I have not entirely erased from my reconstructed soul, but then, **the Doorman of the Century** is after all, a menial post . . . (ARRANT *looks at him.* DANCER *smiles.*) I got the order. (*He jerks his head to indicate a room.*) Down the telephone . . . (*Pause.* ARRANT *unbuttons his neck, opens his coat.*)

ARRANT: What matters to you, Citizen? (*Pause.* DANCER's *eyes are fixed on* ARRANT's *throat.*)

> I said —

DANCER: Love! (*Pause*) So much murder . . . torture . . . the squalor of blighted lives . . . requires some perfect apotheosis . . . to be justified . . .

ARRANT: Justified?

DANCER: Yes, oh yes, you see,

> **The Doorman is a moralist** (*He laughs, stops.*)
>
> No, some impeccable, some — immaculate moment of love —
brief as the metamorphosis which brings to birth the butterfly, perfect, trembling on damp wings and frail as the dew which shakes on the stem — (*He has contrived to place himself behind* ARRANT.)
>
> New in form, and possibly, unobserved —
>
> **Only one such needs occur** (*He grabs* ARRANT *by the head, forcing it back.*)
>
> **For**
>
> **Us**
>
> **To**
>
> **Say** (ARRANT *struggles,* DANCER *slashes his throat.*)
>
> **The sacrifice was perfect** (*They struggle.* ARRANT *chokes.*)
>
> **The sacrifice was more than necessary**

                    We
                    Craved
                    It!
                    Faith!
                    Faith! (ARRANT *lies back in the chair.*)
                    Jane!
                    Where are you!
                    Jane! (*He runs around in a fit of uncontrollable excitement.*)
                    I'm changing! I'm altering! I'm undergoing something **that**
was far from spontaneous (JANE *appears with a bucket.*)

JANE: What!

DANCER: **I plotted every move** (ARRANT *is dying, but noisily.*)
                    Shut up!

JANE: You're mad!

DANCER (*kicking* ARRANT): Shut up, shut up!

JANE: **Mad**
                    Utterly
                    Mad

DANCER: Faith he said (*He jeers at the dying man.*)
                    Faith in me!
                    Finish him off, I can't

JANE: No —

DANCER: **Do it I said** —

JANE: Absolutely not —

DANCER (*going to her, taking her roughly*): You know your trouble —

JANE: Nope —

DANCER: I'll tell you what your trouble is —

JANE: Don't wanna know —

DANCER: **You have no loyalty!**

JANE: Nope —

DANCER: Neither to the past nor to the future, I find that **contemptible**
                    Do it or I'll have you shot

JANE: Rubbish
                    That horrible noise

DANCER: Well, cover him up! (*They stare at each other like a quarrel-
ling husband and wife. Pause.*) All right, I will! (*He goes to throw*
ARRANT's *coat over him, but senses the presence of* CHRISTOPHE.
CHRISTOPHE *pours fluid from his little can.* DANCER *pauses, throws
the coat over* ARRANT. *The sound is muffled.*)
                          I knew him at once
                          The way they
                          Swaggering about as if
                          And staring
                          I don't stare, do I? Tell me if I do I hate it
                          And just arrive!
                          No introductions
                          Good morning would be nice
                          I'm too subtle

For my own good, possibly . . . (*The grunting stops. He looks, shakes his head.*)

And he called **me** the doorman . . .

How little they know of our rareness, and our beauty . . .

JANE: Beauty? You?

DANCER: Yes . . . . Me . . . (*She turns to go out.*)

Jane . . .

I don't know what to do with these . . .!

JANE *shrugs, goes out, leaving* DANCER *alone. The wind makes the boards creak. He hurries to the body and picks up an arm, but the body is if anything, heavier than the last. As he pulls, and falters, he becomes aware of* CAROLINE, *who has returned alone, watching him. Pause. He allows the arm to fall with a feigned indifference. Music, percussive, brief.*

PART TWO

CAROLINE, *alone*. ROMANOFF *is revealed, staring at her . . .*

ROMANOFF: Your shoes are covered in mud . . . (*Pause*)
               Not just your shoes . . . (*Pause*)
               Your legs . . . (*Pause*)
               Your legs are covered in — (*The* CHILDREN *enter.*)
GRISELDA (*seeing the laid table*): What's this . . .!
HELEN: This is the old service from the summer house!
ROMANOFF (*to* CAROLINE): I hate to see you spoiled in any way —
CAROLINE: I'm not spoiled —
ROMANOFF (*hurrying to her, kneeling with a handkerchief*): Horrible —
CAROLINE: Not spoiled, I said —
HELEN: Laid for six . . .
GRISELDA: And the high chair, though Christophe doesn't use it any more . . . !
ROMANOFF: All right, I won't attempt to clean your legs, what does it matter if we are clean or dirty?
HELEN (*to* CHRISTOPHE *who has wandered near the table*): **Don't touch the food** . . .
ROMANOFF (*applying spittle to his handkerchief*): No, I think it does matter, actually . . . (*He wipes* CAROLINE's *legs desperately.*) I think it is supremely important . . .
GRISELDA (*staring at the banquet*): What is this for? If they are going to murder us, what is this for?
HELEN: I think they want to make us foolish. I think it is grotesque and horrible and —
GRISELDA: The food *is* poisoned, I suppose . . . ?
HELEN: **Altogether typical of Mr Dancer**. (ROMANOFF *is working with a passion.*)
         I can see exactly what they want. They want us to sit here in a parody of plenty and then possibly on film, certainly with photographs, to suffer an agonizing death, falling across the table, choking on the silverware — (GRISELDA *bursts out laughing.*) No, it isn't funny, it is the way they think, it is the very essence of their mentality and —
CAROLINE (*who has not moved*): **It's a wedding.** (*Pause. They look at the table.*)
GRISELDA: Yes . . . ! There's a cake . . . !

Pause. They look at CAROLINE. *Music.* DANCER *enters. He stops. It is as if he suffers an embarrassment, and chooses not to speak the thing he had intended. He goes to the chair at the bottom of the table and sits in it, thoughtfully. No one else moves. The wind and creaking woodwork. At last he looks up.*

DANCER: A transient phenomenon . . .
        Celebrates . . . (*He jumps up, clumsily.*)
        Well, that's what we're supposed to do, isn't it? Celebrate! (*He stares at them.*) Revolution has become associated with austerity, we can't have that. The fall of dynasties has forfeited its glamour and become a sordid and obscure transaction occurring in a cellar
        The committee lacks imagination
        I have always said so
        I would go so far as to say it defines the thing . . .! (*Pause*)
        One would think we were ashamed . . . (*Pause*)
        So . . . (*Pause*)
        I am so frightened my greatness may go unremarked . . . (*He gestures for them to sit. They do not respond.*)
CHORUS: **Dancer**
        They will humiliate you
DANCER: Obviously, they'll try . . .
CHORUS: **Four hundred years of power**
        Do you think they'll play with you
        They'd rather die
DANCER: They're decadent. Even the boy.
CHORUS: **Drag them outside**
        One volley and forget
DANCER: That is precisely what I wish to avoid! That is precisely the mundane practice of all revolutions and I think it fails to grasp
        The
        Symbolism
        Of
        The
        Sacrifice (*He looks at* ROMANOFF.)
        Please . . .
ROMANOFF: You are asking me to sit at my own table.
DANCER: Yes.
ROMANOFF: To eat off my own plates.
DANCER: Yes.
ROMANOFF: With cutlery that bears my own initials.
DANCER: Yes. (*Pause*)
ROMANOFF: You are a man of such mean sensibilities I do not think you even comprehend the gravity of your own offence . . .
HELEN: He does . . .
ROMANOFF: Does he . . .! Then he also understands why I will not concede to him the right to extend me such an invitation!

HELEN (*turning away*): I'm sure he does . . .

ROMANOFF: **The servant offers dinner to his master . . .!**

CAROLINE: Yes!

ROMANOFF: **The mutinous tutor invites the prince to eat off his own crockery!** (*Suddenly he sits at a chair.*)

> I am as subtle as you, Mr Dancer!
> Wretch!
> Animal!
> Simian deformity!
> What's the hors d'œuvre?
> It had better be good you cur
> Not that you'd know cuisine from the stable floor
> Insect
> Parasite
> I can play this game
> Any game
> Better than you
> Lout
> Rodent
> Did you think me trapped in regal postures?
> Stiff and fragile?
> Morally obtuse?
> A Fabergé of manners and conventions?
> Inflexible?
> Absurd?
> **No**
> **No**
> **No**
> The laugh's on you (*He gestures to his family.*)
> Do sit
> Do sit (*He spontaneously flings a plate to the floor.*)
> Oh, dear, the family crest . . .! (*He leans across the table violently.*)
> **Monarchy is not material, citizen!**

Pause. DANCER is taken off-guard by this tirade. He stares at ROMAN-OFF, as do the entire family. The CHILD goes silently to his father and takes his hand. Pause. Tears come into ROMANOFF's eyes. Without further instruction, the CHILDREN and CAROLINE take their places at the table. Pause. JANE appears at the door in an apron.

JANE: Do you want it, now? (DANCER *does not reply.*) Look, Dancer, I am not sweating to pieces in the kitchen while you —

DANCER: Shh!

JANE: Make up your mind what time you might or might not —

DANCER: **Shh I said** . . .

JANE: I've got a home to go to! (*She goes out with a cross shrug.*)

ROMANOFF: Servant problem? (*The briefest pause. He does not look up from the table.*) Listen, if you get us out of here I will pay you one hundred and fifty thousand American dollars . . . (*Pause*)

DANCER (*as if abstracted*): Mmm?

ROMANOFF: I said if you —

DANCER: That's nothing to you —

ROMANOFF: No, but a great deal to you —

DANCER: The merest trickle from the great lake of your estate —

ROMANOFF: Very well, five hundred thousand American dollars —

DANCER: Really, this is embarrassing —

ROMANOFF: It doesn't embarrass me —

DANCER: It should do —

ROMANOFF: I have children and a wife to —

DANCER: Precisely, and to save them you are prepared to dispense —

ROMANOFF: Double that figure —

DANCER: To dispense the merest fraction of one part of your annual income —

ROMANOFF: Triple it —

DANCER: The microscopic portion of your wealth you deem appropriate to ransom your so-called loved ones **some love this** —

ROMANOFF: **I deemed it adequate to corrupt a worm like you**.

DANCER (*shouting off*): **We'll have it now!** (*Pause. JANE appears.*)

JANE: Are you trying to be funny, Citizen?

DANCER: I do not have to try. Apparently I bring it out in others

  Do you seriously believe my passion has a price . . .? (*Pause*)

ROMANOFF: Passion? (*The wind. A single note, discordant. JANE goes out.*)

GRISELDA: Father . . . I can't eat . . .

HELEN: Me neither . . .

ROMANOFF: Stay in your places.

HELEN: I want to go to a priest . . .!

ROMANOFF: There is no priest, stay in your places . . .

HELEN: And all this is trickery!

ROMANOFF: Of course it is trickery, but we are not humiliated by the antics of others, History will record how — (JANE *appears with a large tureen. She stands in the doorway. Pause.*) In our ordeal we —

GRISELDA: I am not interested in History —

ROMANOFF: We ignore it at our peril —

GRISELDA: I want a child . . . (*Pause*)

  So what if I'm fifteen? (*She stands.*)

  Mr Dancer

  I think the sins of royalty cannot be extended to the children
                                    of the children of

  Etcetera

  My body has no politics and

  You can be the father if you wish

A great silence, in which the sound of the snoring of CAROLINE *is audible. They look at her, for the first time aware she has fallen asleep.* DANCER *is deeply moved, not by* GRISELDA, *but by* CAROLINE . . .

DANCER: She snores . . .! (*He looks to* ROMANOFF, *in amazement.*)
        Oh, God . . .! She snores . . .! (*He half-laughs, half-snorts.*)
        Impossible . . .!
JANE: Do you want it or not?
DANCER: Jane! She snores . . .!
JANE: So do I —
DANCER: Yes, but —
JANE: Shall I serve it up or —
DANCER: **Shh shh philistine shh . . .!** (*Pause. The sound of sleep.*)
        She dreams . . .
GRISELDA: You're not listening to me . . . (*Pause*)
        Nobody is . . .!
ROMANOFF: Sit still, please . . .
GRISELDA: I can't, I want a child . . .!
ROMANOFF: You will have a child, I promise you —
GRISELDA: How!
ROMANOFF: I don't know yet, sit still . . .
GRISELDA: **Mr Dancer I am prepared to make children for the Revolution**

        Kindly
        Make
        Me
        Pregnant
        Or
        Anybody
        Please . . . (*Pause. She sits, humiliated. Pause.*)
        I cannot understand how your ideas can interfere with the functions of my body

        I am so healthy
        I am so fertile
        My womb is not guilty, is it?
HELEN: He is not listening, Griselda . . . .
GRISELDA: No? What is he doing then?
        I am a princess how can he resist me? (*She laughs derisively.*)
        What's in the tureen? Some ghastly thing, no doubt, no, it's peculiar, this desire to live, do you have it?
HELEN: Yes . . . (*She looks at her sister.*)
GRISELDA: **What's in the tureen, something to make us sick**
ROMANOFF: Shh . . .
GRISELDA: Daddy . . .
ROMANOFF: Shh . . .
GRISELDA: Daddy . . . (*The tureen is placed on the table at a signal from* DANCER. *Pause. He stands.*)

DANCER: I'd like to serve you . . . (*He goes to the tureen and picks up a silver ladle.* JANE *reappears.*)

JANE: Psst! (DANCER *is irritated by the interruption to a rite.*) Psst!

DANCER: What?

JANE: There's another one of those Citizens . . .

DANCER: What!

JANE: Outside.

DANCER: Can't be . . .!

JANE: Came by car . . .

DANCER: **Car . . .!** (*The brutal interruption of the telephone.* DANCER *closes his eyes. It rings again and again.*)

JANE: Shall I get it?

DANCER (*shaking his head*): It's funny, isn't it, you would think, in the chaos of a revolution and a civil war, the complete disintegration of the transport system, the telegraphic networks and the rest of it, such a resolute supervision of the minor executives of the People's Will would be impossible, but no, the contrary is the case, a profusion of messengers, a plethora of orders emanating from every corner, and the paperwork . . .!

I'll see to this. (JANE *goes out. He goes to follow, stops.*)

You'd think I couldn't be trusted. (*He leaves. The* FAMILY *remains at the table. The phone ceases.* CAROLINE *snores.* DANCER *returns, stops in the doorway.*)

They're dead I said. (*Pause*)

He thanked me. (*Pause. He shrugs.*)

A few minutes either side . . . what difference does it make?

JANE (*coming in again*): I'm wrong, there's two of them.

DANCER (*shaken*): Two?

JANE: Two Citizens. High ups.

DANCER: **Two.**

JANE: That's what I said — (ROMANOFF *laughs.*)

HELEN: Be quiet!

DANCER: **Two** . . .

CHORUS: **Dancer . . .!**

DANCER: Yes, I'm here . . .

CHORUS: **Dancer**
       What are you
       Are you a liar?

DANCER: A liar, yes. . .! And infinitely resourceful . . .!

CHORUS: **Dancer**
       Your lies will bring you to the ditch

DANCER: I'm too good a rider, sorry . . .

CHORUS: **History will**

DANCER: **I know all about history, thank you . . .!** (*Pause*)

And as for lies, mine are so thoroughbred they leap the brooks and hedges of your mediocrity. Give me a great lie, and I will be its jockey . . . (*Two* MEN *Enter.* DANCER *turns to face them.*)

Where *is* Citizen Fitch? And not only Citizen Fitch, but Arrant, where is he? I try to cope but all I have is a flock of bleating peasants. (*They look.*)

No disrespect, but we know their limitations, don't we? (*Pause*)

All right, not bleating. Unenlightened. (*He smiles.*)

Are you my assistants, or am I yours? (*They laugh.*)

Yes! That is how it is here, one does not know! One greets in pure ignorance God knows what rank of official! It's as well we have abolished all the old formality!

DENADIR (*looking at the table*): Has one abolished it, Citizen?

DANCER: Oh yes, one has most certainly.

DENADIR: Tablecloths, napkins, silverware . . . one seems to have a soft spot for those, notwithstanding . . .

DANCER (*through his teeth*): One has however, an entirely different attitude to objects which once bore particular significance, commanded particular responses, and so on. It is crucial, Citizens, that we address ourselves not simply to the material, albeit we call ourselves materialists, but to the meanings with which the material is endowed. (*He smiles.*)

DISBANNER: Yer love nice stuff . . .

DANCER: **Don't tilt with me I am an ideologist** (*They stare, puzzled.*)

The Doorman, me . . . (*Pause*)

The title has no meaning for you? I promise you it will. (*He goes to the table.*)

Are you on your way somewhere or —

DISBANNER: Who are these? (*Pause.* DANCER *hesitates, marshals his resources, smiles, in the space of a second.*)

DANCER: Chaos.

I like it. (*They look at him.*)

Chaos.

How it suits me. (*Pause*)

It's my medium. (*Pause*)

But you . . .! (*He walks to the chair where the* CHILD *is seated.*)

Gentlemen, I can see from your expressions you are gardeners at heart . . . (*He suddenly seizes the* CHILD *in his arms and holds his, head in a fixed grip as if he were demonstrating the qualities of a calf.*)

Who's this . . .! (*He laughs.* ROMANOFF *jumps to his feet, shuddering, tense.*)

Who's this, he says . . .!

Look . . .! (*The* MEN *stare.*)

Look, then! (DISBANNER *looks at* DENADIR, *who nods, to authorize him.* DISBANNER *stares at the* CHILD.)

No . . .

I don't call that looking . . . (*He drags the* CHILD *nearer.*)

Stare into his eyes . . . (DISBANNER, *hands on knees, stoops.*)

Do you not know the eyes? (*Pause*)
The shape of them?
The colour?
Oh, Citizen, are you such an ethereal scholar you never stooped to pick up the magazines? (DISBANNER's *eyes meet* DANCER's.)
Not once?
In the dentist's waiting room?
Many a passion has been kindled there . . .! (*Pause. Something dawns on* DISBANNER.)
Yes . . .
This peculiar and distinctive physiognomy is all we loathe . . . (*He shakes his head.*)
Whose humiliation and disfigurement can never satisfy our rage . . . (*He propels the* CHILD *bodily into* DISBANNER's *arms.*)
Kiss him. (DISBANNER *smiles, kisses the* CHILD. DANCER *turns to* DENADIR.)
Here are my papers, where are yours? (*He thrusts his documents into* DENADIR's *face.*)

DENADIR: In the car.

DANCER: Get them. (DENADIR *pointedly declines to examine* DANCER's *authority.*)
When I said kiss him — (*He looks to* DISBANNER.)
I meant once . . .

DISBANNER (*to the family, in a spasm of savage delight*):
I'm treading in your brains you!
I'm wiping my boots on your wombs!
And kicking your eyeballs high into the branches! (*He stops, turns to* DANCER.)
It is them . . .?
Is it? (*He returns.*)
And when I walk away I'll drag your entrails through the gardens . . . wiping bits on twigs as if I'd trod in shit . . . kidneys . . .!
Lung clinging to my ankle!

HELEN: Shut up . . . (DISBANNER *grins.*)

DISBANNER: It is them, isn't it . . .? (DENADIR *goes to* DISBANNER *and mutters in his ear. He leaves smartly, stops in his tracks.*)

DENADIR: Did I hear a telephone, Citizen?

DANCER: In the hallway, Citizen. You dial seven, for the Central Committee . . .

DENADIR *goes out.* DANCER *knifes* DISBANNER, *thrusting his hand over his mouth. Instant music. The* FAMILY *variously rise to their feet, cover their mouths, gasp.* CHRISTOPHE *holds out his can . . . The music ceases as abruptly. A peculiar silence.* DANCER *holds* DISBANNER *in a fatal embrace. In this silence,* CAROLINE *can be heard snoring.* DANCER *listens to this. Then he lowers* DISBANNER *to the ground. The wind, the creaking of boards. The* FAMILY *do nothing but watch. One by one, they sit again.* JANE *enters.*

JANE (*pointing*): He's on the telephone!

DANCER: Help me move —

JANE: No —

DANCER: Please —

JANE: I can't —

DANCER: Jane —

JANE: **Don't want anything to do with History!** (*Pause*)

DANCER: This is not History. This is the opposite of History.

JANE: **Won't help a murderer.** (*She stares at* DANCER. *He appears disconcerted.*)

DANCER: Murderer . . .?

JANE: You! (DANCER *releases a slow, tentative shrug of the shoulders. He looks to* ROMANOFF.)

DANCER: Get his legs.

ROMANOFF: No, and nor will anybody else. (DANCER *looks at* ROMANOFF.)

DANCER: You think the transient phenomenon has run out of luck . . . how little you understand me . . . and how correct it is I am obliged to do everything myself . . . to be suspected by every one . . . and trusted by nobody . . . how splendid I have slipped from human knowledge like a playing card lying beneath a desk . . .

JANE: He's coming . . .! (*She hurries out.* DANCER *goes to a chair and sits, extending and crossing his ankles, and joining his fingers as if contemplatively.* DENADIR *enters, see the body.*)

DANCER: He died. (*Pause*)

His contribution to the future was significant, but brief . . . (*Pause.* DENADIR *looks, coolly.*)

I knew when I saw you, that man was a priest . . .

I knew it, I could smell the clinging odour of the seminary which no rebellion of the will or cleansing of the intellect can ever shift.

Throw open the windows of the soul! Let the winds of civil disorder and the rhetoric of lawyers whirl the pages of the antique books, sheets in the gutter, splintering crucifixes underneath your boots but still — (*Pause*)

No, it's painted on your eyes, some profound antipathy to logic . . . (*Pause*)

Help me kill this lot . . . (*Pause.* DENADIR *stares.*)

The Doorman cannot lift the latch . . . (*The tension is too great for* ROMANOFF, *who stands suddenly.*)

ROMANOFF: We love . . .!

We love each other . . .! (DENADIR *stares at him.*)

Pity us . . .

CHORUS (*quietly, intimately*):

> **Dancer**
> **Can you corrupt the so-corrupted**
> **Dancer**
> **Is it possible**
> **You've met your match?** (*Pause*)

DENADIR: Pity . . .? (*Pause. He walks, stops.*)
      We are replacing that by organization.
CHORUS: **Dancer**
      He is not susceptible
DANCER: We don't know yet . . .!
CHORUS: **Dancer**
      He fathoms you
DANCER: We know nothing yet!
GRISELDA: I think you have such a nice face. (*Pause*)
      Such a nice face and you ought to look after it, it's the face
of an angel. (DENADIR *looks at her.*)
      I think if you were capable of murder it would show in your
face. (*Pause*)
      Perhaps you don't like to have the face of an angel, perhaps
it's a burden to you and you think by doing ugly deeds your face will
change. (*Pause*)
      No doubt angels have a lot to put up with and would happily
conceal it. (*Pause*)
      But it's fate. The weak will always come to you. The weak
and the destitute. Obviously, you'll hate them for it. You will squirm at
their dependence and their whimpering, you will be enraged to know
that your own liberty is trampled on by their persistence but . . . (*Pause*)
      The perfect are unlucky . . . have you not heard the angels
complain . . .? They do! They groan . . .! (*She looks down at her plate.*)
      They grasp at anything which will suffocate the pity that
consumes them . . . (*Pause.* DENADIR *is staring at her. The wind and
the boards.*)
DENADIR: It's true I have wings under my overcoat I hide them obviously I fold them occasionally a single feather drifts to the ground what's
that they say what's that white thing. (*He bursts out laughing.*)
      You parade your sensibility
      **The blood of thousands oozes from beneath your finger-
nails** (*Suddenly he throws down a set of motor car keys. They lie on the
floor, the subject of everyone's gaze. A long pause.*)
      There is a car
      It's parked by the lodge
      A full tank of benzine
      Maps and (*Suddenly he suffers a paroxysm of mental pain
that doubles him. They watch. He sobs.*)
DANCER: None of them drives, unfortunately . . . (*He goes to* DE-
NADIR, *and with a gentleness, runs his hands along the man's arms.*
DENADIR *weeps on* DANCER's *shoulder.* DANCER *kills him with the
knife in this embrace. A cry.*)
      It's better . . .! (*A cry again.*)
      No, this is better . . .! (*And again*)
      The torments of a pure soul!
      I couldn't bear to witness it! (*He staggers, lowers him.*)
      Martyr!

Martyr to an instinct which all life abhors! (*He looks at the dying man, then turns to* GRISELDA.)

Console him . . . (*She is staring in fixed horror.*)

Console him, then . . .! (*She goes unsteadily, kneels, weeps.*)

ROMANOFF: He would have saved us . . .

DANCER: Yes . . .

ROMANOFF: **He would have got us out of here!**

DANCER: Of course he would! I saw it in his eyes!

ROMANOFF: **Then what** —

DANCER: Do you think we have had a revolution in order that idealistic priests masquerading as policemen could indulge an appetite for gestures by liberating oppressors such as you? What do you think the revolution is, a stage?

ROMANOFF: Yes, what else is it? (*Pause.* DANCER *shrugs.*)

DANCER: Yes, and this performance, however predictable, threatened to overshadow me . . . (*He calls.*)

HELEN: You kill people. You just keep killing them

DANCER: Yes, it's so much easier than I thought —

GRISELDA (*holding up a tiny crucifix*): Look! He wore this round his neck . . .!

JANE (*entering*): **What.**

DANCER (*to* GRISELDA): Wear it yourself . . . your eloquence entitles you to some reward. . . .

JANE: **Christ you've gone and** —

DANCER: Both of them, yes —

GRISELDA (*through a sob*): **I caused his death . . .!**

ROMANOFF: Nonsense! All you said was true and beautiful and nothing caused his death but this monster and his delinquency!

DANCER: Excellent. Unfortunately, she is too sophisticated for your platitudes. (*To* JANE.)

Help me move these to the —

ROMANOFF: **I detest you**, Dancer. **I curse you.** (*Pause*)

JANE: You keep asking me to shift these bodies —

DANCER: I know, and you keep refusing, but —

JANE: **I'm innocent and that's how I'm staying.**

DANCER: Do you think I want to kill these people? They keep turning up, one after another, it's like hacking the limbs off a centipede . . .! (*He shudders.*)

Horrible . . .

And their banality . . . their philistine instincts, glamorized by philosophical quotation, their cruelty, legitimized by slogans, they don't know what cruelty is . . .! It's pure savagery to them . . .! Indulgence . . .! (*He shakes his head.*)

It is such a difficult time to love . . . to surpass oneself . . . to triumph over the servile characteristics of a rebellious character like mine . . . and love . . . difficult . . . oh, difficult . . .

CHORUS: **Dancer**
Dancer

> Some lapse some complication
> Makes us distrust you
> We crave their execution and you give them
> Dinner

DANCER: It's no more than a ritual, I assure you . . .

CHORUS: **We demand their deaths**

DANCER: Yes . . .

Yes . . . and the people must be gratified, of course. I feel your breath, hot on my neck . . . not very sweet breath, but sweet breath is almost certainly evidence of degeneracy . . . (*He leans over the sleeping* CAROLINE, *so her breath falls on his face. Silence. A note played. He is ecstatic. Suddenly, he turns and sweeps the car keys off the floor.*)

How fortunate I am I do not need a chauffeur!

ROMANOFF (*standing*): Take us. Drive us to the frontier. Redeem your stunted life by a single act of perfect charity. (*Pause.* DANCER *laughs quietly, shaking his head.*)

DANCER: Do you think I have not thought of that? From the very first day of the uprising, do you not think I anticipated that? Whilst you were scarcely troubled by reports of riots, whilst the disintegration of the army cost you hardly any sleep, I was rehearsing the very moment of your passion, and the role I'd play in it . . .

ROMANOFF: Yes, I believe you.

DANCER: Most men would, of course. The gratification, the celebration, the reputation the everything heroic and magnanimous, who could refuse? (*Pause*)

Only me. (*Pause*)

Unfortunately, I am cursed with subtlety. (*He makes a tremendous throw, sending the keys far into the night. A wind.*)

I have to guard against myself. We all long to evade our destiny . . .

ROMANOFF (*to* HELEN): Come here . . .! Come here . . .! (*She goes to her father, weeps in his arms.*) Griselda . . .!

GRISELDA (*not unkindly*): No . . .

ROMANOFF: Christophe . . .! (*The* CHILD *goes to him. The group rock, tearfully, in each other's arms.* DANCER *watches. Then, to rupture the tension, bursts out.*)

DANCER: Firstly, I mastered the vocabulary. Less than one hundred words, I promise you, is adequate, two hundred makes you an expert, entitling you, to a limited extent, to innovate! Yes, I am a most convincing exponent of the theory of revolution whilst at the same time disciplining myself against the temptation — always present in a man of real intelligence — to intervene in the higher levels of debate — a fatal error because is renders you — (*Pause*) Please stop that — (HELEN *wails.*) It renders you an object of suspicion to the — (GRISELDA *cannot help herself, and wails also.*) Please . . .! (*Pause*) The very individuals you most hoped to — (JANE *now shakes with grief.* DANCER *watches with a peculiar disbelief.*) satisfy . . .

The sound fills the stage, ROMANOFF *himself grieving loudly. In this orchestration,* DANCER *moves, like a fascinated child in a museum of anguish. His delicate steps take him round the table, to where* CAROLINE *still sleeps. He takes her head between his hands and kisses her, deeply, lengthily. Through their grief, the others are slowly made aware of this. They cease, their horrified gaze falling on the spectacle.* ROMANOFF, *repressing an urge to attack* DANCER, *moves away thoughtful . . . watches from a distance*

CAROLINE (*as* DANCER *withdraws his lips*): I sleep — I can't describe the clinical reasons — I sleep to isolate myself — as if like some insect I might undergo a change of such proportions I would not, on waking, recognize myself . . . (*Pause*) I do recognize myself . . . (*Pause*) And the sleep's hell. Perhaps it is for butterflies. Perhaps there is a price to be paid for such brief apotheosis. (*Suddenly*)
      I keep dreaming I'm on trial . . .!
ROMANOFF: I think, this time, there will be no trial . . .
CAROLINE: Pity. I would have conducted myself very well, if the dream is anything to go by. I would not be acquitted, but they would suffer the humiliation of committing a judicial murder. The public would know this, and . . . (*She shrugs.*)
      How romantic . . .! As if the public cared . . .!
HELEN: Mother . . .
CAROLINE: Yes . . . (*She looks to* DANCER.)
JANE: **Let 'em go . . .! Let 'em go, Dancer . . .!**
DANCER: Jane . . .
JANE: **I can't bear this . . .!**
DANCER: It's difficult . . .
JANE: **Bodies, more bodies . . .!**
DANCER: I know . . .
JANE: I try to be historical, I try to be — (*Pause*) to be — what's it —
DANCER: Objective —
JANE: That's it, I do and —
DANCER: You've done splendidly —
JANE: **Children . . .!** (*Pause.* DANCER *looks at her.*)
DANCER: Yes. (*Pause*)
ROMANOFF: Citizen Dancer has a personal interest in this . . . (*He goes to* JANE, *touches her lightly on the shoulder.*)
      Which, even were the ground not thoroughly patrolled . . . would render your pleas meaningless . . . (JANE *wipes her eyes with her sleeve.*) Help me move these dead men out . . . who . . . for all their cruelty . . . were simple . . . raging but possibly also . . . kind . . . (*Pause, then* JANE *assists him to drag away the two dead men.* CAROLINE *goes to* DANCER, *boldly.*)
CAROLINE: You won't escape the consequences of this, Mr Dancer —
DANCER: No —
CAROLINE: On the contrary, you will be the next to be eliminated —
DANCER: Yes —

CAROLINE: The shame of this will oblige them to destroy every piece of evidence, including the witnesses —

DANCER: Yes —

CAROLINE: You and the man who murders you and him who murders him, they all —

DANCER: **I understand that very well** —

CAROLINE: **My life is perfect, look at me**. (*Pause*)

HELEN: Mother . . .

CAROLINE: Shhh —

HELEN: Mother, we are all —

CAROLINE: **I am fighting for my life and you should fight for yours** (*A cold wind, she shrugs.*) Or if you prefer not to, don't . . . (ROMAN-OFF *watches her, having returned from moving the bodies.*)

If you would rather acquiesce . . . with dignity and so on . . . do . . . I don't criticize . . . (*Pause*)

I am not a good mother, am I? I plead for myself, and my humiliation, if it is humiliation, embarrasses you.

HELEN: You shouldn't stoop to such a —

GRISELDA: Oh, let her, let her stoop . . .!

HELEN: **Such a horrible and** —

GRISELDA: I stooped! Stoop yourself!

HELEN: **Never**

GRISELDA: It would do you good to stoop for once —

HELEN: Shut up!

GRISELDA: No, it would do . . .!

HELEN: You'd take your clothes off for this monster, you just said so, what kind of family lets a child — (CAROLINE *laughs bitterly.*)

What kind of family. (*Pause. Slowly,* JANE *goes out.*)

We have offended her . . .

CAROLINE: Yes. The poor cannot bear their masters to be human. *They* can be human, but not us . . . (GRISELDA *grasps* HELEN *in her arms.*)

DANCER: The beautiful exists . . . but only because the hideous exists . . . I am the hideous, and the agent of the hideous . . . I have never concealed it from myself.

CAROLINE: I don't find you hideous, Mr Dancer . . .

DANCER: Please . . .

CAROLINE: I am perfectly serious, I don't find you —

DANCER: **Time's very short**

Too short

For transparent compliments

And the arrière pensée, madame! (*He laughs, shakes his head.*)

I find . . .

How infuriating . . .

I find . . .

So few who are in any sense worthy of great sacrifice, so few, and possibly — one must grasp the nettle — such individuals do not exist, but this does not diminish in the least, the will to sacrifice, misery of miseries, it possibly enhances it . . . (*Pause. He looks at* CAROLINE.)

> I adore you . . .

> And you are — spiritually — poor . . . (*Pause*)

CAROLINE: I resent that, Citizen.

DANCER: Of course you do . . .

CAROLINE: I am beautiful, a princess of royal blood, and you —

DANCER: I am an ugly and mutinous tutor, yes . . . (*Pause*)

> There is a cake there, but where is my bride? (*Pause*)

CAROLINE: I'm here — (*Pause. She looks to her* HUSBAND. *He makes a slight move of his head, encouraging her.* DANCER *puts his hands to his cheeks.*)

DANCER: The innocence of me . . .!

> Even these — (*He indicates the* CHILDREN.)

> Are more —

> Sophisticated! (*Pause.* ROMANOFF *steps forward.*)

ROMANOFF: I'll give the bride away . . . (DANCER *is puzzled. The telephone rings. He is still. It rings and rings.*)

> Shall I?

> Wouldn't you like that? (*Ignoring him,* DANCER *walks out of the room. Pause. They speak at once.*)

> It's all right, I know what I'm doing —

HELEN: Don't quarrel with him —

ROMANOFF: I know his type —

HELEN: Whatever he says, do it —

ROMANOFF: Humour him —

HELEN: Things that horrify or possibly disgust you, still —

ROMANOFF: Grit your teeth and —

HELEN: Crawl, Mother —

ROMANOFF: I never thought I'd say this but —

HELEN: Creep, Mother —

ROMANOFF: The lives of our children depend on the denial of our feelings —

HELEN: Submit —

ROMANOFF: Caroline —

HELEN: Submit —

ROMANOFF: Caroline . . .! (*He stretches out an imploring hand.*) I shall suffer every second of your degradation . . .!

> Every second . . .! (*His hand, extended over the table, is ignored by her. It remains.*)

HELEN: We so admire you . . .! (*Pause.* DANCER *enters, slowly. He walks as if in deep thought, ignoring them. He stops. He turns at last.*)

DANCER: I have been ordered to place myself under arrest. (*Pause*)

> I've done so, obviously. (*Pause*)

> The higher wisdom of the Committee, the exigencies of the Terror, who could quarrel with it? Not me. (*He looks at them.*)

> A Transient Phenomenon expects nothing less than to be

crushed beneath the wheels of Progress. I don't hesitate. I fling myself headlong. (*Pause*)
>Privacy.
>Idiosyncrasy.
>Call it what you like.
>Must be extinguished like a cigarette.
>His words, not mine. (*Pause*)
>The personality is no longer the exotic garden of indulgence but the park of the people. (*Pause*)
>His words, not mine. (*Pause*)
>Gates down. Walls down. The squeals of dirty infants in the summer house . . . (*Pause*)
>My words, not his . . . (*Pause*)
>Really, he has a fine mind, the Citizen at the terminus of all the telephones. And not bereft of sensibility, no . . .!

Pause. It is darker, the evening closes in. The wind blows in the silence. Suddenly, as if in horrible anticipation, CHRISTOPHE *runs from his* FATHER's *arms to his* MOTHER. *She clasps him . . .*

CAROLINE: Shh . . . (*She strokes his hair.*)
DANCER (*looking into the night*):
>Hated nightfall
>As long as there was day
>I sensed the power to distinguish
>Will from appetite
>What thrilled me in the sun
>Is threatening by night
>Hated nightfall
>I'll lie awake all hours
>Plotting injury to those I love
>And you will pass an unclean hand
>Over the eyes of malcontents
>The senile dissidents
>And those
>Who find a recompense in cruelty . . .

Pause. CAROLINE, *steering her* SON *into the direction of his* SISTERS, *goes towards* DANCER, *who gazes into the evening.*

CAROLINE: Save yourself . . . (DANCER *turns to her.*)
>Yourself and me . . . (*He examines her, not without suspicion.*)
>You because you believe in nothing.
>And me, because I represent everything.
>The cynic.
>The symbol.
>Lucidity.
>And illusion.

Take me to a foreign city and we can live as poor as beggars in a room . . .

I will be a mystery to you.

Naked.

On a mattress

Poverty

Exile

And

Desire . . . (DANCER *looks at her* . . .)

My body is not perfect —

DANCER: I've seen it —

CAROLINE: Three children leave their mark —

DANCER: Seen it I said —

CAROLINE: But an empress is an empress and — (*Pause*)

Seen it, how? (DANCER *shrugs* . . .)

DANCER: All night on a balcony . . . nothing to me. . . . soaked to the skin and clinging to a creeper . . . nothing to me . . . (GRISELDA *laughs, stops.*)

ROMANOFF: Wretch . . .! Monkey and wretch . . .! (GRISELDA *forces her hand into her mouth.*)

DANCER: Underneath the curtain an inch of light. . . . adequate for me!

ROMANOFF: Pitiful and melancholy dwarf!

DANCER (*staring at* CAROLINE): And the underwear . . .! (GRISELDA *bursts out again.*)

Yes!

Absurd! (*He looks to* GRISELDA.)

She knows! The tutor scrambling in the laundry, there's religion for you . . .!

CAROLINE (*measured*): If ever a man needed to sleep with an empress, that man is you. . . .

DANCER: Sleep with. . . .? Sleep with, she says . . . as if that mundane act could compass the terrible extent of my devotion . . . how little you know of love, Caroline.

CAROLINE: Instruct me, then . . .

DANCER: How shallow you are . . . as I always knew . . . so shallow it wounds me where I am most pervious to pain . . .

CAROLINE: Teach me . . .

DANCER: I preferred you sleeping . . . then at least I was deceived —

CAROLINE: **Teach me I said**. (DANCER *falters.*)

Night after night. Noon upon noon. Teach me. I have had a life of poverty. Drag me to a room and we will pulp our misery in the pursuit of some smothering ecstasy **drag me**. (DANCER *stares, moved by her vehemence. She tears her dress from the shoulder.*)

This is my flesh and it is dead. Unlit as Arctic winter. Breathe on me.

DANCER (*struggling against her*): Fifteen nights in Paris . . belly to belly underneath the roof —

CAROLINE: Yes —

DANCER: Venice . . . Deauville . . . Longchamps . . . Nice . . .

CAROLINE: Yes —

DANCER: The thrashing of limbs and dreams in mouldering resorts —

CAROLINE: Yes! Yes! Why not! Or on some lonely look-out tower clinging to the cliff where we will caress each other under changing skies with the intense devotion of the archivist . . . (*She stares at* DANCER.) I've not been entered. . . . believe me . . . I'm unrevealed . . . (DANCER *is in acute pain . . . He sways.*)

DANCER: It'll only — it'll simply —

GRISELDA: Do go, Citizen . . . (DANCER *turns, shocked at her encouragement.*) I thought I was unhappy but how small my unhappiness is compared to yours . . . leave us, do . . . Oh, my poor mother! What she says is true! (ROMANOFF *covers his face in grief.*)

DANCER: Yes. . . and the way she says it . . . is the proof . . . (CAROLINE *flings herself on* DANCER, *sliding down to his knees.* DANCER, *profoundly moved, looks at* ROMANOFF.)

ROMANOFF: It isn't too late, Dancer . . . you can go . . .

DANCER (*as if lost*): Go . . .?

ROMANOFF: **Love her and go.**

DANCER *yearns towards* CAROLINE, *but a movement catches his eye.* CHRISTOPHE, *with his watering can, climbs onto the table and proceeds to pour the contents over the cake.* DANCER *watches with fascination. The spell is broken. A low laugh comes from him . . .*

DANCER: That was not the love I had in mind . . . I would lie with the silence of a spent lover and grieve under the seagulls for the apotheosis I had shirked . . . (*He looks to* CAROLINE.) Madame, you —

With a percussive shock, an arm, holding a rifle extended, is thrust through the floor. The rifle is flung down with a clatter. The arm remains fixed in the air. CAROLINE *falls forward onto her hands, sobbing.* ROMANOFF *goes to dash to her.*

ROMANOFF: Oh, Caroline — (*He is stopped by the appearance of a second rifle thrust through and flung down as before. He takes account of it, then goes to* CAROLINE *and places his hands on her shoulders.*)

> I'm sorry
> I'm so sorry
> I'm so sorry
> So sorry
> So sorry

CHORUS: **Dancer**
Forgive us we
Suspected you of
Ambiguity
Lukewarm in your devotion

> **To the future**
> **And inclined to**
> **Clemency** . . .

DANCER: Clemency . . .? But History doesn't know the word. . . .

DANCER *seizes the tiered wedding cake in his arms . . . He staggers under the weight . . . A pipe plays a dance off-key.* CAROLINE *goes to a chair, sits, sleeps.* DANCER *revolves with the cake as the* CHORUS *laugh. His dance takes him past the figure of* CAROLINE.

CHORUS: **Mock her**
> **Mock her**
> **The bitch's garments are woven from our poverty**
> **Humiliate her**
> **She fucked with priests**

DANCER (*revolving*): She did, did she. . . .? (*Some laugh in staccato contempt. Others excite themselves in chanting.*)

CHORUS: **Monarchy**
> **Monarchy**
> **Another word for depravity**

DANCER: You know everything. . . .!

CHORUS: **And the husband was anyway**
> **Completely**
> **Impotent!** (*They laugh derisively.*)

DANCER: I never knew. . . .!

DANCER *falls at* CAROLINE's *feet, clutching the cake. A silence. A wind blows.* GRISELDA *sings a psalm.* JANE *enters, clutching a saucepan.* GRISELDA *stops.*

JANE: There's a woman outside says —

DANCER: A woman . . .?

JANE: A woman yes and — (DANCER *takes the knife from his pocket again.* JANE *is horrified.*)

> Dancer . . . (*She swallows with apprehension.*)

> Dancer, you can't — (DANCER *plunges the knife into the cake. He looks at* JANE, *then at the others.*)

DANCER: My bride's arrived . . . (JANE *stares.*)

> Do share my cake . . . (*He extends a slice.* JANE *is motionless.*) You are afraid . . .

> The consequences of partaking of my wedding cake . . . appall you. . . . (*He tosses the slice. It strikes* JANE *on her apron, falls. . . .*)

JANE: Dancer . . . you are a stupid, stupid man . . .

DANCER (*hacking another slice*): **Let them eat cake!** (*He tosses it wildly over his shoulder.*) She was not cruel . . . she was struggling with incomprehension, Marie Antoinette . . . (*He flings another. Into the silence, a* WOMAN OFFICIAL *of the Revolution. It is as if they all knew her and expected her.* JANE, *desperate, turns to her.*)

JANE: Can I go now?

    I did nothing except when I was forced and even then my soul revolted

    Can I?

    At all times my inclination was to say no thank you

    Thank you I would rather not

    Another time

    Etcetera

    God knows my innocence

    God I love him God (*She closes her eyes. She goes to move.*)

    I'm wiping up, I —

ALBEIT: Stay where you are.

A musical effect. ALBEIT *goes among the family, touching them lightly on the shoulder one by one and indicating they should move to the back of the room. She touches* CAROLINE *last. She does not move.*)

DANCER: She sleeps . . . the Empress . . . (ALBEIT *indicates to the* CHORUS *with a movement of her head. They come and lift* CAROLINE *in the chair.* CHRISTOPHE *goes to his mother.*)

    She sleeps because she cannot tolerate a world whose poverty of spirit includes even her . . .

JANE: **I want to wipe up, please!**

DANCER: Oh, let her wipe up. She is a servant, and they deteriorate without their servitude I've noticed —

ALBEIT (*to the* CHORUS): Arrest this man. (JANE *drops the saucepan with a clatter.*) And her.

DANCER: Oh, Jane, and you did nothing!

JANE: **Done nothing, no!**

CHORUS (*as they jerk* DANCER *and* JANE *into chairs*):

    Dancer

    Some misunderstanding obviously

    Some temporary

    Some

    Some

    Ideological

    Complexity

ALBEIT: Where are the Citizens named Fitch and Arrant, Disbanner and Denadir?

ROMANOFF: Dead! They're dead!

ALBEIT (*to* DANCER): Where are the citizens, I said —

ROMANOFF: He killed them

    He tortured them

    He slit their throats before our eyes

    Abominable monstrosity

    No loyalty to anything exists in that deformed and poi-
soned soul

HELEN: Father!

ROMANOFF: The world revolves and dynasties can come and go but that diabolical and cynical parcel of depravity —

GRISELDA: **Shut up**

ROMANOFF: **Shut up?**
Never will I
Cease in my indictment of — (*Pause*)
Citizen, look in the soup tureen. They were feeding us human remains.

HELEN (*incredulous*): What . . .?

ROMANOFF: Yes, oh, yes, he was up to all sorts of —

JANE: **Human remains?**

ROMANOFF: The heads, yes, hacked them off and boiled them, arms and legs —

HELEN: What. . . .!

ROMANOFF: In the soup . . .!

HELEN: Father!

ROMANOFF (*to* ALBEIT): The ones you mentioned, I don't know their names —

HELEN: Father, please . . .!

ROMANOFF (*to* ALBEIT): **Cleanse the world, Madame!** (ALBEIT *hesitates* . . .)

JANE: What heads . . .? I spent hours finding mushrooms for that soup — (ALBEIT *strikes* JANE *across the face.*)

ROMANOFF: Good . . .! Good . . .!

CHORUS: **Dancer**
Dancer
The vegetables will testify against you
The banquet will rise up and point
An
Incriminating
Finger . . . (*Pause, then* ALBEIT *goes to the soup tureen.*)

HELEN: It's impossible . . .!

ROMANOFF: Shut up.

HELEN: Impossible —

ROMANOFF: Shut up you idiotic child nobody requires your interventions!

HELEN (*aghast*): Idiotic child . . .?

ROMANOFF (*whose gaze is fixed on the table*): That's what I said . . .!

HELEN: I forgive you . . how hard it is but I forgive you . . .

ROMANOFF (*staring madly at* ALBEIT): Good! (ALBEIT *removes the lid of the tureen. She looks in. She calculates. She replaces the lid.*)

JANE: There you are, now you can see what's what I'd like permission to — (ALBEIT *silences* JANE, *taking her face between the fingers of one hand menacingly and twisting her.* JANE *is still. Her head hangs.* ALBEIT *walks up and down.*)

ALBEIT: Chaos . . . (*Pause*)
How it licenses depravity . . . (*Pause*)
And we, constructing on the ruins of the past a new society,

encounter in the strangest places exotic delinquencies . . . (*She looks at* DANCER.)

> Cannibals
> Perverts
> Amoralists

ROMANOFF: **Abandoned by God and reviled by man . . .!**

JANE: Cannibals?

ALBEIT: Old and rotting systems whose debauched relations bring to birth in their senility transient phenomena such as this . . .

ROMANOFF: **Cleanse, Madame . . .!**

JANE: What cannibals . . .?

ROMANOFF: **Cleanse . . .!**

DANCER: Oh, how they hate me, Jane . . . in this, these arch-opponents are of one accord . . . for I am the antithesis of History, which has manacled their souls . . . (ALBEIT *seizes him by his hair and forces back his head. At once, the* CHORUS *flock to observe his ordeal.*)

CHORUS: **Dancer**
> **Dancer**
> **We feared you would display this** (*He lets out a cry.*)
> **Arrogant**
> **And**
> **Petulant** (*He cries again.*)
> **Disharmony . . .!**

JANE (*horrified*): Leave him . . . leave him . . .! (*He cries again. The* GIRLS *cover their mouths.*)

ROMANOFF (*in a rambling, disonnected tone*): We were tired, obvious-ly we were tired, but it was not just tiredness —

HELEN: Don't die . . .! Don't die, Dancer!

ROMANOFF: No, I think one must acknowledge tiredness such as ours owed something to the greater lassitude of God, I think God Himself was tired — (DANCER, *concealed behind the gathered* CHORUS, *lets out a profound groan . . .*)

> I think His silence was the withdrawal of His love which possibly we had ceased to value . . . and in consequence He turned — not far — the slightest averting of His face is after all, sufficient for the eclipsing of all happiness —

GRISELDA: Shh!

ROMANOFF (*mildly now*): Shh . . . why?

The CHORUS, ALBEIT, *stand back from* DANCER. CHRISTOPHE, *irresistibly drawn to* DANCER, *slips off his* MOTHER's *lap and silently peers at him.* JANE *extends her hand to hold* DANCER's . . .

JANE: Dancer . . . Oh, Dancer. . . . that woman's blinded you . . .

GRISELDA: We love you . . . We love you. . . .!

HELEN: Yes, oh, yes . . .!

DANCER (*croaking*): Yes. . . . I know you do. . . .

ROMANOFF: Oh, Dancer, what are you . . . **What are you . . .!**

DANCER: Afraid . . .

ROMANOFF: Afraid . . .?

DANCER: Afraid death even . . . will be poorer than my imagination predicted. . . .

ROMANOFF: **Our souls will meet in paradise!**

GRISELDA: Yes! Yes! And Mr Dancer will be — oh, will be —

HELEN: Content!

GRISELDA: Content at last!

JANE: It's all right, Dancer . . . it is . . . even if it seems. . . . not right. . . . at all . . .

ROMANOFF: **I take him in my arms!**

GRISELDA: We all do! We all do! (DANCER *is aware of* CHRIS-TOPHE's *proximity. His head turns to him* . . .)

DANCER: Listen. . . .

   Listen. . . .

The wind blows. The sound of CAROLINE's *snore.* CHRISTOPHE *lifts his watering can and pours the contents over* DANCER's *uptilted face* . . .

WOUNDS TO THE FACE

CHARACTERS

A WOMAN AT A MIRROR
A MAN
A SURGEON
A SOLDIER
A MOTHER
A LOVER
A BRIDE
A PRISONER
YOUTHS
MONSIEUR
A VISITOR
A WIFE
A TERRORIST
A SECOND TERRORIST
A DICTATOR
A DOUBLE
A SECOND DOUBLE
AN EMPEROR
AN EMPRESS
A PAINTER
A GUARD
A ROUÉ
A PROSTITUTE
A SECOND PROSTITUTE
NARCISSUS
A GREEK
A SECOND GREEK
A PATRIOT
A WOMAN WITH A PARASOL
A MAN

FIRST, TO LOVE YOURSELF

A WOMAN *at a table and mirror. The litter of make-up. She works. She suffers. She flings down some tool with vehemence.*

WOMAN: An hour I've been here! (*Pause*)
An hour . . .! (*Pause*)
Firstly, there is no point, none whatsoever, in disputing what cannot be dissented from, the face is the face, what I was given, what I came into the world behind and which it is impossible to disown or disassociate myself from, we are implacably united dreams notwithstanding, tastes, opinion notwithstanding, no, it's this and no other, start from the facts, live with the facts and stop this futile and nauseating, **Oh, God, an hour**, dissidence! (*Pause. She looks. Suddenly she grabs up a pencil.*)
An hour so what! I am not content to endure without protest the severe injustice of being trapped behind, no, gaoled in, yes, **incarcerated** in a face I have profound objections to, I refuse to yield to circumstances I was not party to, I register my disobedience! (*Pause*)
More than an hour now . . . (*She peers into the glass.*)
I do not like it. Never did I like it. Not from my first look did I and having said so perhaps I now might lay aside my just criticism of God, His idleness, His wit, His sarcasm and so on and proceed to — (*Pause*)
I cannot move from this stool . . . (*Pause*)
It is quite possible I shall never move again from off this stool because I cannot reach agreement with my face, I cannot make a compromise or an accomodation with my face to live and let live, no, we hate each other and it clings there like an uninvited insect I will not walk into the world behind this thing I actually detest, how did I get like this, an hour ago I was nothing like this **I've missed the train the bus and the connection**. (*Pause*)
Really, this mirror gives me more trouble than a dozen children, violent husbands, anything, perhaps it lies, mirrors do lie, it's possible a different mirror would convey a different picture, wholly possible, this mirror is against me and reflecting falsely **I accuse mirrors yes because they are dishonest** everybody knows, one says one thing, one says another, I am tired of being made a fool of **into the garden and throw a brick at it** or if it's not the mirror it's the lights, my position vis-a-vis the window, a dozen things might influence what

I am seeing and consequently what I am seeing is by no means truth but some distortion, I have allowed myself to suffer a distortion! Idiot! (*She laughs.*)

Really, an hour and a half for nothing . . .! (*She picks up a tool. She cranes. A* MAN *is discovered observing her.*)

MAN: An hour and a half today . . . not bad . . . some days she spends an entire morning there, and never once lifts her eyes higher than the mirror's rim. I observe, and am not observed. (*Pause*)

At first, this pleased me. I was gratified by my own cunning, privileged to see and be unseen, but now . . . (*Pause. The* WOMAN *gazes at herself, with a studied objectivity.*)

The opposite because what are her efforts for if not for me? I cannot tolerate such an expenditure of effort on the creation of a face that exists apparently for itself alone, I am offended, I considered breaking her window with a stone, or more subtly, in a faked accent telephoning, and with an affectation of concern, announce she is not so solitary as she believes herself to be, a catapult would do it, look, I am exposed to my full-height in the window and still . . .! (*Pause*)

Blind . . .!

Spontaneously, the WOMAN *weeps with rage and disgust. Three placards simultaneously descend, identical images of the face of the* DICTATOR. *A gang of* YOUTHS *rush in and attack the placards, defacing them. A sound of an explosion, as of a grenade. A* SOLDIER *enters, whose face is swathed in bandages except for the mouth. The* YOUTHS *hurry away, shouting.*

SOMETHING CAN BE DONE IN ALMOST EVERY CASE

A SURGEON, *white-coated, enters. He looks for a long time at the still figure of the maimed* SOLDIER.

SURGEON: I am not insensitive. How hard it is to hold, however. How hard. Always ready to take flight, an anxious bird which trembles in the hands. Some don't. Some can't. I however, try. (*Pause*)

Your jaw has gone, and one half of your face, the eye included. The nose, entirely, and the mouth, the palette, a cavern now. You feel this damage, and the scale of it. I have never seen a worse case but there have been worse. A worse case always. Raise your hand if you follow me. (*The* SOLDIER *raises a hand, lets it fall.*)

And we have such skills now, such infinite resources, our aim is to restore you to the level of a tolerable life, a complex notion, I agree, one might dispute its meaning, raise a hand if you can follow me. (*The* SOLDIER *does so, lets it fall again.*)

The face is after all, a structure, it is a particular organization of muscularity and bone, fibre, membrane and if never replaceable, it can be reproduced, and if not made identical, similarity can be achieved, say if you follow. (*The* SOLDIER's *hand rises and falls.*)

Some wars ago, before photography, the remade face was pure speculation, therefore a work of art, whilst technical, also a field for dream, but now we have so many images to hang our efforts on, one might say we improve on the authentic **you will be forever hideous and sit alone in rooms** . . . (*Pause. The* SOLDIER *raises his hand.*)

They hover in the corridors of Europe, behind avenues of trees, and do not talk. Ghosts have little need of conversation, you will find . . . (*The hand falls. The* SURGEON *goes to the* SOLDIER.)

And did she whisper how she loved your face, and with the tender touch of adoration trace your brows, brushing your lips with hers and swimming hour after hour in your gaze, and in the darkness find assurance in the contours of your face? (*The* SOLDIER *is silent.*)

That's all for today. I expect we shall see much of one another from now on. (*He starts to go out, but senses the* SOLDIER *has raised a hand. He stops, without turning.*)

Yes, kill yourself if you wish. I would. (*He goes out, passing an aged* WOMAN, *who looks grievingly at the* SOLDIER.)

MOTHER: What does he say . . .? (*Pause*)

My son, what does he say?

SOLDIER: I am not the only one.

MOTHER: No, but —

SOLDIER: High walls and trees, he says. (*Pause*)

MOTHER: And what about —

SOLDIER: Benches. Gravel in the gardens. And fountains, possibly . . .

MOTHER: Yes, but —

SOLDIER: But conversation not to be anticipated, apparently —

MOTHER: **The face, what of the face, my son?** (*Pause*)

SOLDIER: No face, Mother. There's none. (*A long pause. The* MOTHER *suffers, braces, determines.*)

MOTHER: Then you will need me. For a man without a face will earn no love from women. On the contrary, they will shudder, and love will come from me alone, me, the solitary source again . . .! (*Pause*)

My breasts tingle! (*Pause*)

My breasts . . . dear one . . . (*A* MAN *enters, looks at her.*)

YOU WILL ENDURE ME, LONG AFTER I HAVE GONE

LOVER: I was looking at your photograph! (*He smiles.*)

The peculiar fashions of your youth . . .! And even, it seems, a way of smiling, which is almost certainly the smile of a period, the smile of twenty years ago, I am not sorry you have aged, you have shed a certain shallowness and gaiety with the years and now your beauty is quite painful to behold, dead vanity, and the ruins of an arrogance lend you such dignity, it is as if you were disappointed, not once, but over and over again, which I find attractive, perhaps peculiarly, and you are lucky, I suppose, to have acquired me as a lover at your age . . .

MOTHER: Lucky, and I never cease to think it.

LOVER: When I could find any number of mistresses whose eyes were sky blue with undamaged life . . . (*He unbuttons her.*)

MOTHER: I sometimes gasp at my good fortune . . .

LOVER: What do people think, I wonder, seeing me visit you?

MOTHER: They do see, do they? I thought, by visiting me at night, you spared them the embarassment of speculating on the subject . . .

LOVER: It is clandestine, but of necessity . . .

MOTHER: I understand that, I was not criticizing you — (*The* LOVER *kisses her passionately.*) Not criticizing you at all . . .! (*She embraces him. He sinks onto her.*) Sleep now . . .

LOVER: How much I want to . . .!

MOTHER: Sleep, and I will wake you. Have I ever let you down? Always, I arouse you in time.

LOVER: Yes, you do . . . and yet . . . sometimes I feel I cannot read your face . . . suppose you love me but . . .

MOTHER: Love you . . .! Do I *love* you . . .? (*Pause*)

LOVER: Too much? (*Pause*)

MOTHER: Possibly. (*She smiles.*) I often think, possibly this love is too great for the normal world . . .

LOVER (*scoffing*): The normal world! God forbid the normal world!

MOTHER: God forbid it, yes! (*She lowers his head.*)

     Sleep now . . . (*The* LOVER *sleeps, blissfully. She kisses his face, taking from her skirts a thin, cruel blade which she suspends over him. Again, she kisses him, and then plunges it fiercely. He emits a terrible cry.*)

     You carry me, the consequences of me now, I cannot be denied . . .! (*He rushes from the room.*)

     If I bear age, then you bear temper! We wear each other's pain . . .! (*Sobs from offstage. The* LOVER *returns, a towel over his face. He is still.*)

     Sorry.

     Perhaps you can boast one day of the madness you induced. Ridiculous face.

     Goodbye. (*The* LOVER *is still.*)

LOVER: Help me.

     Help me, I have a wife!

MOTHER: Go to the wife, then. (*The* LOVER *peers over the towel.*)

LOVER: I'll say I was attacked.

MOTHER: Yes, say that. Shall I call a cab?

LOVER: By men. Attacked by men for no reason.

MOTHER: It happens all the time.

LOVER: My handsomeness offended them, I'll say . . . they marked me for no reason . . .

The LOVER *goes out, slowly. A mirror descends in front of the chair on which the* SOLDIER *is sitting. He stares.*

THE PERIMETERS OF AN OATH

The MOTHER *stands behind the* SOLDIER, *and then, with an effort of will, begins to unravel his bandages. At last he is exposed. They both stare into the mirror. Their horror, their will, suspends them. A knock on the door.*

MOTHER: Don't come in. (*Pause*)
       Or come in. (*Pause*)
       Don't . . .! (*Pause*)
       Or do, if you want . . .

A young WOMAN *enters. She goes to the mirror and stands behind the* SOLDIER. *A long pause.*

THE BRIDE: I can't marry you now . . . (*Pause*)
SOLDIER: Someone threw a grenade, but badly . . .
THE BRIDE: Now now . . .
SOLDIER: Instead of landing in the enemy, it bounced back . . .
THE BRIDE: Not now . . .
SOLDIER: It hit a post, and bounced.
THE BRIDE: I cannot . . . now . . . I cannot . . .
SOLDIER: If the post had not been there. Or if the weather had been different. If I had been more agile. Or if his nerves had not spoiled his aim. (*Pause*)
       Another would be faceless and I. (*Pause*)
       Of course I think this all the time. (*Pause*)
       What if the post had rotted in the rain . . .?
THE BRIDE: Always philosophical. . . .
SOLDIER: The same man. The same.
THE BRIDE: I
       Cannot
       Marry
       You
SOLDIER: The same but in different proportions . . .
THE BRIDE: **One loves the outside, forgive me, the outside also**. (*Pause*)

SOLDIER: I do think this piece of wood has much to answer for. Its effects on your character, for example, I wonder where —

THE BRIDE: Forgive me, I said . . .!

SOLDIER: Where this post is now . . . As they carried me away I tried to mark the place, this post was in my mind, it possibly exists still, holding up a barn door and not significantly decayed, it rains on this post and in summer it grows warm in sunshine . . .

THE BRIDE: I cannot lie beside you now . . .

SOLDIER: And then I think, this post was once a tree, and had a crop of leaves on, oak or beech, how I should like to lie beneath its arching bough, in your arms, obviously . . .

THE BRIDE: **Please say you understand** . . . (*Pause*)
         I would so like to take that understanding away with me.
. . . (*The* SOLDIER *is still, silent.*) By witholding that, you are not philosophical at all . . . (*Pause*)

SOLDIER: Now I am particularly exercised if it was pine or beech the post which like a cricket bat so deftly drove the bomb into my face . . .! **Not oak, I think**, we exhausted oak in the war's first year **understand you say** oh, always understand, the world is thick with the slippery paste of mutual understanding, understand yes, which is not forgiving is it, I understand the post, but forgive it, no, we cannot marry it is an outrage to decency, obviously . . .

THE BRIDE: **I loved your face and it has gone**. (*She turns to go. She encounters the* MOTHER's *gaze.*) How you hate me, and will never speak of me again, I know. But there are women like me everywhere, uttering this same pitiful revulsion in a dozen different tongues . . . (*The old* WOMAN *smiles grimly.*) How you make me hate you for that look . . . (*She goes out. A* WOMAN *in prison garb enters, stands with a mirror in her hand, but resolutely avoids seeing herself in it.*)

MOTHER: They all want forgiveness! But we are unforgiving! We walk along the middle of the road! Horror! Horror! Ring a bell to make the children hide! That woman and her awful son! She had one life, and now she has another! He had one face, and now he has another!

ARBITRARY IMPRISONMENTS

The PRISONER *holds the mirror at arm's length, turning it cruelly towards herself and then averting her face to avoid the image. She repeats this action from another angle, yearning towards it, recoiling, laughing with fear and relief. She drags a worn photograph from her pocket, examines it, stuffs it away.*

PRISONER: Twenty years in a hole. (*Pause*)

Twenty in a hole **it can be done** and I was not resilient.
(*Pause*)

In a pit open to the sky never mind the reason and then the tide came in, it always does, eventually the tide comes in bringing the dead on its crests but also the living **leave your hole** a voice said and put a hand down which I took, the greatest handshake in the world I defy you to propose another, twenty years in a hole, it can be done, and for no reason, probably my face, my face was hated by someone **or loved possibly loved** that also was a reason for denunciation **loved by someone and therefore doomed to a hole** I understand that — better I was in a hole than gave myself to others oh, I understand that passionate possession, twenty years, twenty without a mirror. (*She holds up the photograph.*) Of course I've changed. Not necessarily, but very likely I have changed, the climate in that hole, it varied from freezing to suffocation, so hardly do I entertain the idea I am recognizable, no, this is quite — (*She suddenly tears up the photograph and scatters it.*) The face of a dead woman to all intents and — (*She drags the mirror past her face, shrieks, closing her eyes at the crucial moment to avoid seeing her image.*) I am such a coward! Such a flagrant! And I rubbed shit into my flesh! This was for warmth initially, I wore it, I weaved it into rugs, was there ever a parallel desire to exist, I was an insect but not quite an insect for I obviously harboured **vanity!** (*She thrusts the mirror beneath her and sits firmly on it.*) **Can't look!** But possibly, were I to look, and obviously I will look, the moment will certainly announce itself, I'd be less horrified than I anticipate because the peculiar conditions in which I've lived, the characteristic properties of holes and bogs might have — I speculate — **preserved me** — don't mock it happened to some Celts their bodies were as perfect as the day they or Romans possibly no Celts it was and underneath the crust of my endurance the youthful face of unused beauty still — (*Bawling off. Three placards of the dictator descend. The* YOUTHS *burst in, tearing and ripping the images.*) He's dead, then?

YOUTH: Yes, and all the holes filled in!

PRISONER: Dead, and I thought he was immortal . . .

YOUTH: Every morning, his mug in the classroom!

SECOND YOUTH: Every morning, in the workshop!

THIRD YOUTH: And on the bus, his mug bore down on you!

PRISONER: So there was one thing good about the holes, for twenty years I never saw it . . .! (*She cackles. The* YOUTHS *start to run away.*) Don't go . . .!

YOUTH: We're off to rip his mug off other walls!

PRISONER: Wait! I've also got a face . . . (*They stop.*) Describe it, would you?

SECOND YOUTH: Find a mirror —

PRISONER: I have a mirror, but I'm afraid to use it!
Don't go I suffered. (*Pause*)

YOUTH: A nose. In the middle. (*They snigger.*)
And underneath, a mouth . . .

PRISONER (*with a bitter smile*): Very good . . .

SECOND YOUTH: Either side of the nose, an eye — (*They giggle again.*)

PRISONER: That's perfectly good to start with —

YOUTH: Ears. Teeth, I imagine — (*She bares her lips.*)
        Teeth, yes —

SECOND YOUTH: (*mockingly*) Teeth . . .!

PRISONER: And old?

YOUTH: Teeth rather —

PRISONER: **Old or not?**

YOUTH: Dirty, certainly —

PRISONER: Ignore the dirt —

YOUTH: Dirty and —

PRISONER: **The dirt's a crust . . .!** (*She drags a cloth from her clothes, spits on it and begins to scrub her face.*)
        Don't go . . .!

YOUTH: All people from the holes look identical to me! (*The* YOUTHS *hurry off.*)

PRISONER: **Only a crust!**

NOT ABSENT, HIDDEN MERELY

An ARISTOCRAT *of the seventeenth century enters, wearing a velvet mask. He bows to an elegant woman* VISITOR *who observes him.*

MONSIEUR: The Bastille is a world. (*He sits.*)
        Huge, this world. (*Pause*)
        It is a grave mistake to think the plains of Africa are wider than this room. (*Pause*)
        Of course this knowledge comes only to him who most requires it. (*Pause*)
        Is that not the case with all knowledge? It grows on grief. A mould. A bacillus. And very floral, sometimes. (*Pause*)
        Also, I sleep a lot. (*Pause. He laughs.*)
        Laughter in the Bastille
        Yes
        Plenty of it
        Don't believe everything you read . . . (*Pause*)

THE VISITOR: You have such a beautiful voice.

MONSIEUR: That too, I cultivated here. Prior to my sentence I slurred my speech.

THE VISITOR: Such a perfect voice a woman might adore you for it . . .

MONSIEUR: Or a man. The gaolers ask me to recite. In exchange they bring me innocent requests. Soap. Scissors. Pencil stubs. And the mask is not uncomfortable. The Venetians who made it measured every feature with infinite care. Alas for them, because they had seen me they were put to death. No one living has observed me since. (*Pause*)

THE VISITOR: Remove the mask. (MONSIEUR *laughs*.)
          Remove it, I have a longing to kiss you.

MONSIEUR: Only in solitude am I allowed my face.

THE VISITOR: This is solitude — (*He laughs*.)
          Don't laugh at me . . .!

MONSIEUR: No, it is I who is foolish, for believing solitude exists. I am constantly observed. Sleeping, defecating, in sickness and in health, my unseen mother watches over me.

THE VISITOR: How can they punish you, or I, for that matter. It would not take so very long, this kiss. Men and women die for less.

MONSIEUR: The penalty is not extracted from me, but from others whom I love. (*He stands, with a swift, nervous movement.*) Beyond this sanction, nothing much offends me here, no one is ill-disposed to me. After all, it is not me they hate, but the identity. Not what I am, but who I was, and that is beyond all repair and alteration. **I should like to kiss you also** never mind never mind I always say that never mind the words are written on my ribs and I once put them to music —

THE VISITOR: Make love to me!

MONSIEUR: I said it is impossible to slip my mask —

THE VISITOR: In the mask then, and let the watcher watch. (*Pause*)

MONSIEUR: No. (*Pause. The* VISITOR *glares at him*.)

THE VISITOR: No? And are you so supplied with lovers you disdain to —

MONSIEUR: I have no face, and cannot make love, therefore. (*Pause. She shrugs*.)

THE VISITOR: I will imagine your face. And what I imagine will be commensurate with all I have conceived this passion for.

MONSIEUR: **I cannot be imagined when I am**. (*Pause. He smiles. He shrugs*.)
          I mean . . . I **am**. . . .

THE VISITOR *drags her skirt over her head with an impulsive gesture, and is still, fixed to the spot.* MONSIEUR *watches her, agonized. At last, with a movement towards her, he goes to tear the mask from his face. A* VOICE *booms from a hidden place.*

VOICE: Keep the mask on please, Monsieur . . .! (MONSIEUR *stops in his tracks*.)

MONSIEUR: Yes . . .

VOICE: All right, Monsieur, thank you . . .

Pause. Three placards of a dictator descend. The YOUTHS *rush in to deface them. The* SURGEON *is passing in the street.*

WE PUNISH THE PICTURE

The SURGEON *stops to watch.*

SURGEON: The real face. That also must exist. But where?

YOUTH: Cut his moustache off, so the radio said, and hiding.

SURGEON: A single plane left here this morning.

YOUTH: So what? We'll send assasins.

SURGEON: And plastic surgery? I somehow think he won't remain like that . . .

YOUTH: Exterminate the surgeons! (*The* YOUTHS *laugh.*)

SURGEON: Yes, well, that's one solution . . . (*He joins the* SOLDIER *and his* MOTHER. *He takes off his hat.*) Nice day! The birds indifferent to the revolution, evidently, since they sing the same old tunes . . . (*He undoes his bag.*)

SOLDIER: I lost my face for one regime, perhaps another will give me another . . . (*He laughs brutally.*)

SURGEON: Sardonic humour is a most benign resource to those who cannot come to terms with meaningless pain. I frequently encounter it.

SOLDIER: **My lover quit**.

SURGEON: Did she? And am I supposed to be indignant? Isn't it enough that I have to probe the ruins of your physiognomy, but I have to listen to your grievances as well?

SOLDIER: I only mention it . . .

SURGEON: And when your mother dies, you'll tell me that, I suppose? (*He opens a book.*) Now, here you see some faces I have saved. (*He flicks through.*) I say saved. Saved from what? They are not saved, they are inventions. Not one gives me the slighest satisfaction, though many call them miracles. (*He selects one.*)

      Regard this miracle. Him I distinctly improved, but you were handsome, you started from altogether higher principles, which is why I recommended suicide . . .

MOTHER: We are so grateful! We thank God!

SURGEON: Do you? Why? It's me you should thank.

MOTHER (*peering at the book*): This gives us hope . . . (*The* SURGEON *looks at her.*)

SURGEON: You are weeping . . .

MOTHER: Yes . . . because so much is bad . . . and yet . . . there is still good . . .

SURGEON (*looking at the book*): Him I did badly. Him I felt antipathy towards . . . (*He tears out the picture, screws it up.*) When one rebuilds the face, one rebuilds the character. It's inescapable.

SOLDIER: I'm staying as I am.

SURGEON: And this reconstruction of the soul is yet another maiming, we must be frank . . .

SOLDIER: **As I am with all respect**

SURGEON: The forcing of a character into the mould of altered features, what a journey, what an epic . . . I watch . . . I gasp . . . (*He thrusts the book back in his bag.*)

Stay as you are, yes. Flaunt your bitterness. Make them squirm who, if they did not cause your pain, are guilty certainly, of painlessness . . . (*He thrusts his hat on his head.*)

Good day! (*More placards descend and are attacked. To* YOUTH).

Found him yet? They say he's in the city, after all.

YOUTH: They're hunting for him in the sewers!

SURGEON (*moving on*): The sewers! That's where he belongs!

The YOUTHS *laugh. The* SURGEON *passes through. The damaged* HUSBAND *appears in a door. He holds the cloth pressed to his face.*

SHE KNEW AT A GLANCE

LOVER: Darling . . .!

Help, darling, help . . .! (*A* WOMAN *appears, is filled with horror.*)

THE WIFE: What . . .!

LOVER: It's all right . . . it's all right . . . it's — (*The* WIFE *lets out a cry.*)

Not much . . . just a — just a — (*She walks slowly to him.*)

Slash over the face . . . (*She removes the towel. Her hand goes to her mouth to stifle shock. He presses the towel back.*)

THE WIFE: Why . . .?

LOVER (*shaking his head*): No reason.

Louts.

Did not like it.

Louts . . .

WIFE: Louts?

LOVER: Did not like my face, presumably.

Drunkenness and.

WIFE: Did not like your face . . .

LOVER: **It has to be punished this drunkenness**

What are we

Walking down a street and

What are we

I said no

No I said

I was so inoffensive

We must live abroad we must

A country with no louts

Or fewer louts

WIFE: Did not like your face, why ever not?
LOVER: **Why me I said**
        I'm inoffensive
        We do not like your face they said
        Not face I don't think another word
WIFE: Not like your face?
LOVER: That's what I said
        Can you get another towel or bandage
WIFE: **Not like your face it's incomprehensible**
LOVER: Of course it is it's drunkenness it's what louts do it's every-
        where it's
WIFE: Your face is beautiful (*The* LOVER *stops.*)
        Your face is perfect. (*Pause*)
LOVER: To you. But not to others, evidently, wash me I am caked in
        blood ... (*The* WIFE *stares. Pause.*)
WIFE: It is not possible that anyone would spoil your face. (*Pause*) It is
        perfect and would command the silence even of a drunkard whose
        dislocated soul oozed hatred for the world ... (*Pause. The* LOVER
        stares at her.) I know that face. It is inviolable. And never could be
        marked by malice. (*Pause. He shrugs.*)
LOVER: So you say but —
WIFE: Not by malice. Only love.

The LOVER *stares. A* FIGURE *enters in a hood and goes to sit at a
dressing-table.*

THE HOLY ORDERS OF A TERRORIST

TERRORIST: Killing today. (*He plucks his hood, adjusts it.*)
            Killing today and my hood took her eight hours. Eight
hours' labour! What a tailor! What a perfectionist that woman is the
stitching is what she calls Flemish Flemish stitch she says, running the
tape measure around my face, do you want the top to peak or topple fold
or stand up proud, perhaps to hug the contours of your face, these things
are fashions, too, some years ago they were all wool, but now, a vast
selection of materials and linings, too, what once was simple and ex-
pedient is now the subject for individual taste, style, even eccentricity,
so she did this and I approved it, I approved it at the drawing stage. (*He
stands up, pulling his jacket close.*)
            Killing today and I already famous the subject of some
ballads though ballads are no distinction in these parts the film script
is a far greater compliment but I place little faith in admiration,
what was it Alexander said, Alexander the Great, sycophancy is the

mongrel at the heels of power, I don't call myself another Alexander but (*He stops. He leans on the table to look closer into the mirror.*)

Killing today and that little feeling which I have learned to call a flower growing in my lung the very last of nerves and most important after all to keep a little fear, the traces of an inhibition, cultivated, to be so very cold would mock the passion that inspires bravery. (*Pause*)

Killing today and I'm not alone. (*Pause. He laughs. A second hooded* FIGURE *is seen by him in the mirror.*)

Are you for me or against me? (*Pause*)

Oh. (*He sits.*)

You're ill-disposed and what a lovely morning. Are you the enemy or envy? (*Pause*)

It is so pretentious not to speak, it is so louche, or is your voice a poor thing, peep peep, does it go, a broken reed? All right, stay silent, I'm sure I've met you something in you tells me we're acquainted, come on, take the hat off, son. (*Pause. The* FIGURE *is still.*)

Oh, what a lovely day and my own children on their way to school, my three daughters, I never liked those lunch boxes with pictures of the Royal Family on, if you think I will plead for my life you are mistaken, I am the subject of a dozen ballads and a film in preparation in America, three lovely girls my wife she plaits their hair and spotless you should see the washing line on Monday mornings a dozen little dresses blowing in the wind **have you got a face or not** (*He rips away his own hood.*)

And first thing this morning I thought someone else was doomed **Three lovely girls orphaned by a faceless man** I do love your ambition I had ambition once boys will be boys let a man know who his executioner is **what is it shame or something**? (*He laughs. Pause.*)

I'm at the end of my life, then. (*Pause*)

I have a girl friend in the Monastery Flats you know her probably give her the full account the way I did not flinch or cringe do me that favour will you **what does it matter if I recognize you now** so what too late too bad too everything **you are one man aren't you one man and not another** be a human being have a face . . . (*He turns in his chair to face the intruder.*)

Don't obliterate it . . . don't . . . (*He turns his temple towards him.*)

Just here . . . one round is adequate . . .

Oh, don't obliterate it, don't . . .!

Three placards of the dictator descend. The YOUTHS *rush in, proceed to deface it. They hesitate, sensing the presence of a stranger. This* STRANGER *has the dictator's face.*

THE DICTATOR'S DOUBLE

The YOUTHS *turn, incredulous.*

DICTATOR: He no longer looks like that. (THE YOUTHS *slowly gather about him.*)
>And never did. (*They peer.*)
>The face was a creation. (*He smiles.*)
>You know the way they work. Experts. Photographers. Psychiatrists. Utter fiction. You wouldn't know the real man if he stood in front of you. And that's power, the sheer and staggering effrontery of power, you'd think he would have said 'so what, my mug's my mug, love it or else!' But no. He went and had it manufactured, that's the only word, the Department of Social Propaganda manufactured it **oh, the experts in that building** you know the big one by the river, the brains and skills assembled in that place, philosophy, astrology, sociology, it's not his face at all it's the **Official Image**. (*Pause. He smiles at them.*) And a face like that does not arrive without controversy, I assure you. The committee came up with a dozen options, none of them truthful, none of them the least bit representative, but what's that got to do with it, no, it was a scene of bitter wrangling, and he was relatively innocent, he was — imagine it — the victim of their arguments, he had a headache after twenty minutes but it took **six weeks**, after all the face was doomed to reproduction, stamps, marriage licences, even in the Gonhorrea clinic, and not one was really him, it was **a farrago of approximations** — (*They suddenly menace him.*)
>Pol — ice! (*He laughs, shaking his head.*)
>This is ridiculous, if I was him, do you think I'd go about in this moustache, first thing to go, and the hairstyle, I'd have shaved my head, if you want to know I am the newsagent from Casca and a well-known idiot — (*They lurch to seize him. He tears off the MOUSTACHE. They stop in their tracks.*)
>William.
>The idiot
>And newsagent. (*Pause*)

YOUTH: Asking for trouble, William . . .

DICTATOR: It must be trouble that I want. And I've met others! (*They shake their heads and go off, passing the* SURGEON. *The* DICTATOR *replaces his moustache.*)

SURGEON: Good.
>It won't work twice of course . . .

DICTATOR (*shrugging*): Got newspapers to deliver . . . (*He starts to leave.*)

SURGEON: A little surgery . . . makes all the difference . . . (*He stops.*)

DICTATOR: Surgery? I like my face. It haunts them. It is a masterpiece of wit and coercion. How they need it! How they justify their misery by it, their failures, their stunted lives, let them employ it, it is an icon and an alibi. What do you want me to do? Sit in a Swiss hotel with benign features? I would not deprive them, it is our mutual creation, we made it together, I the inflicter, they the endurers, now, give me away why don't you, join the crowd, how gratifying to hate the already hated, long live the common opinion, let's all dance . . . (*He turns to go. The* PRISONER *enters with her mirror.*)

PRISONER: I'm going to look . . .!

DICTATOR (*indifferent*): Are you . . .

PRISONER: **I'm going to look!**

DICTATOR: Look, then, who cares? (*He goes out. The* SURGEON *remains, watching.*)

PRISONER: I count to three and — (*She holds out the mirror, shutting her eyes.*)

I count to three —

It's got to be done at some point, obviously —

SURGEON: Has it, why?

PRISONER: Shop windows, puddles, sooner or later I will catch a glimpse, so it's better I'm prepared **One!** Most important that I have at least a modicum of self-control, my destiny and so on **Two** a little bit a little under my control **Three!** (*She opens her eyes. She sees the mirror. She drops it. She sways. Pause.*)

I've gone. (*She looks at the* SURGEON.)

I've gone.

SURGEON: What's the matter? Don't you like the face?

PRISONER: Not my face.

SURGEON: Not yours?

PRISONER: My mother's. And I've gone . . .

Sound of traffic. Two MEN *enter from either side of the stage. They stop, catching sight of each other.*

THE NECESSITY OF FULL POSSESSION

They stare into each other's faces. They laugh with bewilderment. The laugh dies away. The FIRST DOUBLE *launches himself violently against the* SECOND. *They struggle, moving first one way, then the other. They cease, exhausted.*

FIRST DOUBLE: Even the eyes are the same . . .!

SECOND DOUBLE: It occurs all over the globe and why it should enrage you I can't think, surely a cause for celebration if anything given the number of human types a miracle, I find it amusing personally, and that hurt my neck . . .

FIRST DOUBLE: You've got to die.

SECOND DOUBLE: Don't be ridiculous, it happens all over the globe . . .

FIRST DOUBLE: I couldn't care less about the globe, the globe leaves me indifferent, I am not influenced one way or another by the behaviour of others here or elsewhere on the globe, do not appeal to me on grounds of what is tolerable elsewhere, I detest you and you must die —

SECOND DOUBLE: How can you detest me, you don't know me —

FIRST DOUBLE: **You have my face.**

SECOND DOUBLE: Or you have mine —

FIRST DOUBLE: No, you have my face, I said —

SECOND DOUBLE: Anyone would think I'd stolen it —

FIRST DOUBLE: That may well be the case —

SECOND DOUBLE: **Ridiculous . . .!**

FIRST DOUBLE (*menacing him*): You are not continuing to exist with a face that does not belong to you, you are not posturing and preening and presuming to walk the streets with a face that is not your own, impostor . . .!

SECOND DOUBLE (*unnerved*): Wait . . .! Please . . . let's just . . .

FIRST DOUBLE: **I claim the face! And yours is fraudulently obtained!**

SECOND DOUBLE (*moving back*): The same could just as well be said of —

FIRST DOUBLE: **I claim it!** (*He flings himself cruelly on the other.*)

SECOND DOUBLE: Oh, God . . .! (*They struggle, vilely, to and fro. At last, exhausted, they come apart again.*) This is madness . . . madness!

FIRST DOUBLE: **Give up your face** . . .

SECOND DOUBLE: Utter . . . madness . . . (*He tries to escape. The other holds him.*)

FIRST DOUBLE: I am stronger than you, or if not stronger, more deter-mined. You are conciliatory and I am not, and that alone ensures I will eventually overcome you and kill you, so —

SECOND DOUBLE (*wailing*): What have I done . . .!

FIRST DOUBLE: You've done nothing, but the injustice of it alters nothing. Wail as much as you like but you cannot keep the face —

SECOND DOUBLE: Mother . . .! Oh, Mother . . .!

FIRST DOUBLE: Yes, they are to blame! So much to blame for every-thing . . .!

With a cry the SECOND DOUBLE *attempts to bolt. Roaring, the* FIRST *pursues him offstage. An* EMPEROR *enters. He looks at an easel, which is covered by a cloth.*

HE SAW HIMSELF, OFFICIALLY

As he gazes, the EMPRESS *enters. She stops. She gazes. She laughs.*

EMPEROR: Moment of truth. (*The* EMPRESS *goes swiftly to tear aside the cloth.*)

Don't yet, thank you! (*Her hand is suspended in mid air. It falls.*) Moment of truth . . .

What does that mean? I love the phrase, but the meaning? **It had better be good oh God it had.** (*Pause*) Perhaps we won't see it today. Perhaps today the conditions are not perfect for truth to announce itself. I personally believe truth comes better on some days than others, climate, digestion, all sorts of things might influence its — (*A* PAINTER *enters, stands patiently. Pause.*) I chose you. Knowing fully. Utterly apprized. Laid myself prostrate before your merciless and scrutinizing brush **am I not a hero** how many kings would yield themselves to someone with a reputation as sour and uncomplimentary as yours? Have you flayed me? Have you whipped me, humiliated, ridiculed? Let me say before you tear away the cloth I shall not destroy it nor consign it to a cellar, I fear contempt, no man more, but what I chose I also submit to, the most powerful man in the world must acknowledge there is no immunity from judgement however unsound that judgement may be, please show me what you've done. (*The* PAINTER *pulls away the covering. The* EMPEROR *goes to look. A very long pause.*)

EMPRESS: May I? May I also? (*The* EMPEROR *goes, looks out of a window. She walks to the canvas. She walks away, slaps the* PAINTER's *cheek. He winces, nurses the place. The* EMPRESS *goes out.*)

EMPEROR: I'm sorry. My wife is impetuous.

PAINTER: Now I'll be murdered, I suppose . . . some hired lout will carve me in an alley . . .

EMPEROR: Shh . . .

PAINTER: Not the first time some enraged female has —

EMPEROR: Shh . . . shh . . .

PAINTER: You say shh, but I've been beaten in the past and —

EMPEROR: Beaten?

PAINTER: Beaten yes and my fingers trodden over for less offence than —

EMPEROR: You are an ill-used man, a martyr —

PAINTER: People who cannot stomach truth should not commission pictures! (*Pause*) My hands were in bandages for weeks . . . (*He shrugs.*) So what, it's a dangerous profession.

EMPEROR: I'll have it hung at once, and the public granted access. Let them troop by and arrive at their own conclusions. (*The* PAINTER *bows, and goes to leave.*)

It is such an ugly thing. (*He stops.*)

You know it is.

And hurts me like a lash.

PAINTER: We entertain such high opinion of ourselves. (*He goes to leave again.*)

EMPEROR: Kiss me. (*Pause*).

PAINTER: Kiss you . . .

EMPEROR: Yes. I am the Emperor and I want to be kissed. (*The* PAINTER *goes to kiss his cheek.*) Not there. (*Pause*)

PAINTER: Where?
EMPEROR: My arse, of course.
                    Is it not also a face?
PAINTER: I prefer not to.
EMPEROR: What's preference? (*The* PAINTER *cogitates.*)
PAINTER: I won't do that. (*Pause. The* EMPEROR *walks a little.*)
EMPEROR: I think you want to overthrow the State.
PAINTER: No, I am merely a —
EMPEROR: **My face is the State. You have attacked my face**. (*Pause*)
    That's treason.
PAINTER: No, I regarded this commission in the same light as —
EMPEROR: Please, no false innocence —
PAINTER: As — as —
EMPEROR: This disingenuousness is not becoming —
PAINTER: Any face which has — certain characteristics and —
EMPEROR: There are faces and faces —
PAINTER: Faces and faces, yes, two eyes, a nose —
EMPEROR: Imperial nose —
PAINTER: A mouth and —
EMPEROR: **Imperial mouth** —
PAINTER: In a particular configuration —
EMPEROR: **Imperial configuration** —
PAINTER: You don't allow me to finish my —
EMPEROR: **You cannot paint an Emperor as you would a bar tender,
    that is a bar tender**. (*Pause*)
PAINTER: The way I saw — the way my eyes read the subject was —
EMPEROR: Treason. The eyes committed treason, even if the will was
    loyal . . .
PAINTER: What do you want to do, then, blind me?
EMPEROR: Yes. (*Pause*)
PAINTER: I'll do it again. (*He goes to cover the painting.*)
EMPEROR: No, that's silly —
PAINTER: Yes, I'll do it now. Come here and stand by the window —
EMPEROR: That really is —
PAINTER (*manoeuvring him*): I see you differently, already differently,
    the light here is so much more — **pencils!** And half-profile, that full-
    face was —
EMPEROR (*shaking him off*): **Absurd!** (*Pause. The* PAINTER *smiles
    thinly.*)
PAINTER: Quite. (*The* EMPEROR *smiles also.*)
EMPEROR: Obviously you did your duty to yourself.
                    There is no quarelling with your integrity, and I would never
    stoop to wreck a work of art, **for that is what it is**. (*Pause*)
                    On the other hand, I am the subject, I have an investment. I
    am not meat on a slab, am I, nor trees on a hill, I am not inert matter, and
    you have injured me.
PAINTER: Perhaps, after all, I should simply kiss your arse . . .? I am not

a good man. I merely have a gift. This gift's a sickness, and it's cost me dear.

EMPEROR: I am so injured, you must suffer for it, anything else would smack of compromise.

PAINTER: Destroy the painting, then . . . !

EMPEROR: Never. It is a work of art. (*He claps his hands. A* GUARD *appears.*)

Blind this man.

PAINTER: **What**
What
Oh what

EMPEROR: One of us must be blinded. Either I must be in order not to see what you have shown me of myself, or you, in order to be blamed for a truth that never should have been permitted.

PAINTER: Lock me in a room but let me keep my sight!

EMPEROR: But it's a burden to you, you said so yourself —

PAINTER: In some ways, but —

EMPEROR: Without eyes you will not be led into such dangerous representations, and yet, being an artist by instinct you will perhaps produce things with your fingers and these may be, unlike your paintings, a celebration of mankind, loving, charitable things, the bitterness having been discarded during your long passage through pain . . . it happens . . .

PAINTER: Yes, it does happen, but —

EMPEROR (*he nods to the* GUARD): I think it's best . . . (*The* PAINTER *screams, crawls.*)

PAINTER: Oh, let me, let me lick your arse . . . !

EMPEROR (*covering his eyes*): Shh! I cannot bear it! Shh! (*The* GUARD *drags him away.*) And you'll be a legend! (*He goes, crying.*) Which is more than I shall be . . . (*The* EMPRESS *enters. The* EMPEROR *looks at the portrait again.*) I think when one is portrayed as a beast, one must be a beast, or the world's a — (*A terrible cry, off.*) Nonsense, surely?

EMPRESS: If only he had told the truth . . . which is that you are kind . . .

EMPEROR: Yes! And had he done so, I should, in character, have been kind to him!

THE ECSTASY OF THE UNREPENTANT

The WOMAN *at the dressing table. She works with a lipstick. The* MAN *observes.*

WOMAN: I crept. I hugged the shadows of the shops. But still they persecuted me. I wanted one thing only — not to be observed. But this desire merely seemed to draw attention to me. They knocked into me.

MAN: Impossible.

WOMAN: They collided with me out of malice.

MAN: Imagination.

WOMAN: **Not so, then! One commanded me to smile!** (*She glares. She returns to her mirror.*) My misery offended him. I said my father had just died. This appealed to him. This seemed plausible. (*She tosses down the lipstick.*) **Rose it says, I don't call that rose!** (*She covers her face.*)

MAN: Oh, listen . . . listen, I find you beautiful . . .

WOMAN: It's not enough . . .

MAN: You must be reconciled to your appearance.

WOMAN: I will be reconciled. When you are reconciled to your poverty, I will be reconciled to my ugliness. (*The* SOLDIER *enters, bandaged. He stands observing her. She observes him in the mirror. She begins, irresistibly, to laugh.*) Oh, it is the war wounded. Oh, it is the man who has no face at all. Oh, and I am in for some moral education. Oh, and oh, again! (*She turns to face him.*) You have found a new career. You are going to be an itinerant exemplar. Surely an asset to the entire community, for who would groan at their condition, having once set eyes on you? You leave repentance in your wake, and the poor are reconciled to poverty and the unhappy obliged to confess they do somewhat exaggerate **not me however**. (*The* SOLDIER *just looks.*) All these lipsticks . . . but it can't be the colour, only the shape . . . (*He extends a hand to her. She sees it, does not respond.*) No . . . it's false . . . it's false!

The MAN, *embarassed, humiliated, goes to assist the* SOLDIER, *who dismisses him with a savage movement of the hand. The struggling* DOUBLES *pass over the stage, desperate, with appalling cries. The soldier's* MOTHER *enters.*

MOTHER: My son! My little one! You do wander! You do stray! Tea-time now and buns the ones with icing on, or the custard-filling, you say!

SOLDIER: How I wish that you had died instead of me.

MOTHER: Yes. I too, wish that.

SOLDIER: I would not hesitate to put you in my place.

MOTHER: Nor I to stand in it.

SOLDIER: You pulped. Not me.

MOTHER: Yes.

SOLDIER: You raw. Not me.

MOTHER: Indeed.
            Indeed.

The MOTHER *extends a hand to lead the* SOLDIER. *He obeys. As they depart, a* ROUÉ *of the eighteenth century enters. His coat is smothered in identical photographs of himself as a child.*

I WAS NOT ALWAYS THUS, BUT ADORABLE

The pleasure gardens of the Palais Royal.

ROUÉ: Here again. Tonight I planned to read. But I've read everything. So I redesigned the garden. But this I accomplished in no time at all. Here again, therefore. And looking for the face that might postpone my death. Certainly I should have stayed in the library. Or wrote a little thesis on Etruscan urns. Certainly I have made the same mistake again. And I was warned! The authors of the ancient world were unanimous and vehement as to the futility of my, the pathos and absurdity of my, but still I, always I, **here again, ladies!** (*A* PROSTITUTE *laughs.*) Yes! Ridiculous your game, and ridiculous mine!

PROSTITUTE: Gloomy tonight.

ROUÉ: In a cheerful way.

PROSTITUTE: Gloomy in a cheerful way.

ROUÉ: That's the benefit of culture, madame, but move along, I'm not absorbed by you and standing there you might obstruct another meaningful encounter.

PROSTITUTE: You don't like women, excellency . . .

ROUÉ: No. But what man does? I adore them, isn't that sufficient? (*The* PROSTITUTE *turns to go.*)

I had a lover once. (*She stops.*)

PROSTITUTE: So you say, on each and every —

ROUÉ: Loved and loved in return, are you interested?

PROSTITUTE: Heard it before, sir —

ROUÉ: Of course you have —

PROSTITUTE: Same old story —

ROUÉ: Same old coin, and how beautiful she was . . .!

PROSTITUTE: More beautiful than me —

ROUÉ: Undoubtedly, a face which was —

PROSTITUTE: The rarest combination of ancient cultures! (*Pause*)

ROUÉ: Yes, exactly, how well you put it, how succinct . . .! And she married a man of such pleasant manners —

PROSTITUTE: More pleasant than yours —

ROUÉ: Much more pleasant, yes, a man who cherished her and brushed her hair . . .

PROSTITUTE: Dark hair . . .

ROUÉ: Which I might have . . . plucking the grey, and letting those fall to the floor . . .

PROSTITUTE: Thirty years —

ROUÉ: Thirty years, yes, sleeping like children, belly to arse . . . (*Pause. The* PROSTITUTE *kisses him, pityingly.*)

PROSTITUTE: Ten pounds . . .

ROUÉ: Not cheap to tell you a story! But I appreciate to keep a straight face calls for uncommon qualities! Anyone new tonight? (*He pays her.*)

PROSTITUTE: The new! The new! Always the new!

ROUÉ: The new contains the fallacy of hope! **It was wrong, I should have married her**. Because in truth, she was spoiled also, by his kindness. All lives are wrong. All lives . . . (*He sees a young* WOMAN.) Is your life wrong, Miss? (*She stops.*) Not seen you before.

SECOND PROSTITUTE: Never been here, sir.

ROUÉ (*going to her*): If my face horrifies you, forgive it, I pay well, ask her.

SECOND PROSTITUTE: It doesn't.

ROUÉ: No? Not horrify you? Fifty years of wrong decisions **that must make the young recoil**!

SECOND PROSTITUTE: No, sir. (*She points to the snapshots.*) Who's he? (*He shrugs modestly.*) Sweet face that boy.

ROUÉ: He had, and blushing . . .! No girl was ever like it, so much shame and tenderness struggled in his cheeks **is thirty pounds agreeable**?

PROSTITUTE: He has some funny tastes, His Excellency does —

ROUÉ: Funny tastes, yes, I speak and make love with my eyes open, kiss me. (*Pause. The* SECOND PROSTITUTE *goes to kiss his face.*)

No!

Not him.

But me . . . (*He extends the photographs on his lapels. She obeys.*)

Oh, lucky youth! Oh, delirium! **Kiss me again**! (*She does so. He gives her some of the money.*)

The disbelief! He has no breath, the breath has left his body . . .! **Kiss me again . . .**! (*She kisses the photograph a third time.*)

I so love to witness his confusion! You lure him from his studies, what's **Horace to a whore's arse**, after all, when you are eleven? Mutter things! Whisper! Make his life **impossible**!

SECOND PROSTITUTE (*addressing the photograph*): You are a very charming boy — (*The* ROUÉ *passes her a note.*) And with such a *serious* expression!

ROUÉ: Go on . . .

SECOND PROSTITUTE: Those lovely eyes which must have come from your mother . . .

ROUÉ: From her, who else . . .

SECOND PROSTITUTE: They bore deep into me and make me feel quite naked . . .!

ROUÉ: Yes . . .

SECOND PROSTITUTE: Do you like me very much? And want to feel me underneath my clothing? Put your hand here if you want to, do you want to, and are afraid I'll stop you? I shan't stop you . . . (*The* ROUÉ *gives her another note.*) Not too quickly . . .! How your hand goes burrowing and your eyes are still severe . . .! Your eyes say one thing and your hand is — oh! Not yet quite familiar enough with —

ROUÉ: **What can never be familiar . . .** (*The* SECOND PROSTITUTE *kisses the photograph spontaneously.*)

SECOND PROSTITUTE: Already you want to meet again! Already you are planning the next occasion! (*She kisses it again and again. The* ROUÉ *is weeping silently.*) My beautiful . . .! My never innocent . . .! (*She is suddenly self-aware. She gets up. She tucks the money away.*)

ROUÉ: Come again. . . . he's always here . . . (*The* SECOND PROS-TITUTE *goes to leave, turns, kisses his mouth with spontaneous adoration.*)

SECOND PROSTITUTE: Idiot! Oh, idiot . . . !

Three placards descend, already defaced. The YOUTHS *rush in, and throw a noose over a beam. Others drag in the* SURGEON, *bound.*

THE ABOLITION OF BEAUTY IN THE INTERESTS OF
SOCIAL HARMONY

SURGEON: The Revolution is diseased! I declare this publicly, the sick-ness of the Revolution is upon us! If surgeons are liable to execution, who is safe, surely the limits of insanity have been passed, I am the hero of the hospitals! What am I guilty of?

YOUTH: The mockery of God.

SURGEON: Even the language is archaic! Mock who? How mock?

YOUTH: You have been tried in accordance with —

SURGEON: I have been condemned in accordance with nothing! What civilized —

SECOND YOUTH: We are not civilized, you are —

SURGEON: The healer is murdered for his powers!

YOUTH: You are not a healer. You are a critic of God. And if cosmetic surgery is civilization, we rejoice in the restoration of barbarity! Noose, Citizen! Beat the drum!

SURGEON: I have given happiness where only misery prevailed! Ask any of my eight hundred patients, what nature so illiberally scattered my craft repairs. The ugly praise my name!

YOUTH: There are no ugly. (*Pause*)

SURGEON: No ugly? Are there not?

YOUTH: Not from today. Nor beautiful. Only the will of God. (*The* WOMAN AT THE MIRROR *throws down her cosmetics.*)

WOMAN: Yes! Long live the Revolution!

SECOND YOUTH: What's beauty but a word? And you cut flesh, for a word. Cut the dictionary instead.

SURGEON: Wait . . . the word exists . . . because the thing exists . . .

YOUTH: Not any more! (*He takes the* WOMAN *by the face, firmly, presenting her to the* SURGEON.) Deny her perfection in the eyes of God.

SURGEON: The eyes of God? God's blind. It's Man who discriminates —

YOUTH: **Is she not perfect**? Say! (*Pause*)

SURGEON: I am bound to say . . . my taste obliges me . . . to confess some doubts about —

YOUTH: **One more time I ask you. Is she perfect, Surgeon, Critic of God**? (*Pause*)

SURGEON: There is a man somewhere would find her so.

YOUTH: **Noose**! (*The* YOUTHS *go to tighten the rope round the* SURGEON's *neck. The* SOLDIER *appears, leading his* MOTHER, *whose face is swaythed in bandages. He stops. He points to her*.)

SOLDIER: She — (*He shrugs*.)

She — (*They observe him. His face is undamaged*.)

It's love . . . (*He shrugs again. A* YOUTH *of Hellenic beauty enters, playing a reed pipe*.)

THE COLLABORATOR RESERVES PART OF HIMSELF

NARCISSUS: Girls pester me . . .

ROUÉ: Obviously . . .

NARCISSUS: Girls fall ill for me . . .

ROUÉ: I should fall ill myself . . .

NARCISSUS: And die . . .!

ROUÉ: That's as it should be. Love's unhealthy. (*He picks up his chair and starts to leave*.)

NARCISSUS: Where did you get that awful face? (*The* ROUÉ *stops*.)

ROUÉ: Awful . . .?

NARCISSUS: Rotted and disintegrating —

ROUÉ: Rotted?

NARCISSUS: Pitted, grooved, and —

ROUÉ: Pitted, me?

NARCISSUS: Wreckage of a face, it chills my bone, it makes my mouth go dry **please look away I'm sorry your glance is like a curse . . .**! (*The* ROUÉ *bows, turns, walks slowly out*. NARCISSUS *taunts him*.)

I know what you are thinking!
The
Compensations
Of
Senility
How do you get that scaly stuff around the eyes?
And that crust of yellow skin?

As for the eruptions . . .! (*He chokes with laughter. He goes to put the pipe between his lips. He detects the presence of a* STRANGER, *who holds an unusual box under his arm. Pause.*)

The Greeks were overcome by the Barbarians, who swarmed over their land, burning, looting, cutting off hands, and because the Greeks were beautiful, they hated them, and made a box. (*A* SECOND STRANGER *enters, waits.*)

Some say the Barbarians were too ignorant to make this box themselves, but some Greek did it, out of spite, a renegade who hated his own race and was perhaps himself imperfect in the face. However, the box was invented and its efficiency recommended itself to the Barbarians, whose first enthusiasm for disfiguring had been spent. The sad fact is, had this box never been invented, rather few Greeks would have had their faces maimed, because hate and envy always die down in the end, whereas this machine was light and practical, transportable, and in the hands of experts, has left its mark the length and breadth of the land . . . (*He looks to the* STRANGERS.)

I've got a dispensation. (*They are not persuaded.*)

All right, you want to see it. (*He puts a hand into his pocket.*) Fuck.

Never mind, they all know me.

Narcissus. (*They stare.*)

Oh, dear, you are feeling menacing today. I'm the royal boy, all right? Your king is my — (*He gestures.*)

All right? (*They take a step towards him.*)

Listen, if you put that fucking thing on my bonce you are in for a — (*He feels again in his pocket.*)

Got it! All right? (*He shows the card. They stare contemptuously.*)

Look, I don't know who you geezers are, but when this gets back to my good friend the Most High and Mighty King of the Barbarians you can start to panic, he won't be greatly pleased and might decide to box your heads for all I know —

GREEK: Shut up. (*Pause*)

NARCISSUS: Oh, fuck you're Greeks . . .

Fuck and fuck again . . .

Look, lads, what's this about?

SECOND GREEK: Be sensible. It won't take long. (*He walks forward with a wrist strap.*)

NARCISSUS: Hold it! I think you — **hold it it I said**! Letting you blokes wander round like this, untrained and so on — (*The* MAN *clasps his wrists.*)

Mis — take! Mis — take!

SECOND GREEK: It only takes a minute.

NARCISSUS: Please, I am exempted from the Face Programme!

The GREEKS *hold him in a tight grip and place the box over his head. Cries come from within. One of the men takes a handle from his pocket and inserts it in a slot. He is about to turn it when a cry comes from offstage.*

PATRIOT: Hey!

GREEK: It's Narcissus, the bumboy and collaborator! (*The* PATRIOT *goes to the box, slides back a panel, sees the occupant, shuts it again.*)

PATRIOT: Yes, well done, now take it off.

GREEK/SECOND GREEK: **Take it off?**

PATRIOT: Yes. No matter how much he deserves it. (*An outraged pause.*)

GREEK: Turn the handle, John!

PATRIOT: **Remove the maiming box.** (*The* GREEKS *are reluctant.*)

GREEK: This roving, poncing youth of utterly degenerate and diseased character has betrayed his people by copulating with the Barbarians whilst our people lost their faces **apparently he laughed**!

NARCISSUS: I never!

GREEK: **Laughed** while boys and girls screamed in their villages **the countryside is smothered in maimed children turn the handle**!

PATRIOT: Wait! And listen!

GREEK: I would rather die than not do this. I have followed him for fifteen days. I will do it or kill myself and that's an oath. And now you have a dilemma because if this bastard is allowed to keep his face I'll hang myself, tell that to the Greeks. (*Pause*)

PATRIOT: You do not question my love of the Greeks, I daresay? I need not provide you with my credentials?

GREEK: Nope.

PATRIOT: So I address you from **the very summit of our principles**. This youth Narcissus is the most beautiful who lives, and in his features lives the essence of the race called Greek, there is no finer specimen **hideous as his character through weakness and ambition is**.

GREEK: Who denies it? It makes me want to turn the handle twice as fast. (*He goes to it, but draws it from the socket, playfully slaps his hand.*)

　　　　I respect you, and I hope you will respect me also . . . he has to suffer, or I will, and I'm innocent.

PATRIOT: This youth is more, and greater than himself. Precisely for his beauty he is immune even to just revenge.

GREEK: **And he is privileged, the whore! Is he not gifted by the Gods but we go further and heap forgiveness on the** — (*He shakes his head, speechless with bitterness. A cynical laugh comes from inside the box.*)

PATRIOT: Yes, it will always be thus, and we must swallow bile again . . . (*He nods to* SECOND GREEK, *who removes the box.* NARCISSUS *rubs his eyes, looks at the* GREEK.)

NARCISSUS: I thought you said you'd hang yourself . . .

PATRIOT: The most beautiful Greek is the whore of the Barbarian . . .

NARCISSUS: Yup.

PATRIOT: Still a Greek, however . . . (NARCISSUS *goes to leave.*)

NARCISSUS (*stopping*): When you lot win . . . I'll be yours . . .

PATRIOT: Quite so . . .

NARCISSUS: Don't take too long about it. Narcissus, he also spoils . . .

THE SOLDIER'S CRUELTY IS RESERVED FOR HOME

The SOLDIER *looks at the* MOTHER, *who is still with resignation.*

SOLDIER: It's what you wanted. (*Pause*)

(*Pause*) And I must not allow my sense of gratitude to spoil my life.

Which it could do. (*Pause*)

The sacrifice being so — (*He shrugs crossly.*)

(*Pause*) **There is something so complacent about you, Mother**.

The fact is I think I have to flee from you. I think to see you there, parked by the fireside day and night, I — (*Pause. Exasperation seizes him.*)

You were not buying love, were you? Is love a bargain, then? **You haunt me and I must be free**. (*The* BRIDE *appears, standing silently in the door. Pause.*)

Twice she's given birth to me . . . and would do, over and over again . . . (*The* BRIDE *extends a hand, a command.*)

Pain and more pain . . . the evidence of love . . . (*He turns to go, hesitates, goes to his* MOTHER *and kneels by her.*)

Let me tell you what your pleasure is . . . to know I walk the world in a decent obscurity, and no eyes follow me, but the eyes of women who would have me share their beds. **Dote! Dote on that your triumph, Mother**! (*He seizes the* BRIDE, *and with infinite, particular, incredulous solicitude, exposes her body.*)

MOTHER: Breathless . . .! (*The* SOLDIER *stops, his hand poised.*)

mother.) Anticipates! (*He turns to look at the bandaged face of his*

Soon!
Soon she!
Murmurs!
Limbs all
Weeping
Hair all
Plunders
Weeping
Pleading
Not yet
Pleading
And

Pause. The SOLDIER *removes the belt from his trousers and without haste proceeds to strangle his* MOTHER. *The* WOMAN *enters.*

WOMAN: The surgeon's dead (*Pause. She watches indifferently.*) I had mixed feelings. On the one hand so much talent, so much skill. Nullified.

On the other, did he not fix on hope like some vile crow? Not that my opinion weighed with them! (*The* SOLDIER *drops the belt. He takes the* BRIDE *in his arms, passionately. They run off, hand in hand.*) No, they were hell-bent! They were deaf to arguments! (*The* YOUTHS *pass, noisily.*)

YOUTH: Throw away your lip-sticks!

WOMAN: I will do!

SECOND YOUTH: In the bin the rouge and the mascara!

WOMAN: Funny words! (*They go.*)
            Obscure properties!

The WOMAN *goes to the mirror. She looks. A* WOMAN *with a parasol enters a garden.*

PERHAPS SHE LIED. BEING INVISIBLE

The WOMAN *with the parasol turns, perambulating. A* MAN *enters, observes her a long time.*

MAN: If you lie, I shall know . . .

WOMAN: Yes. And that is why I turn my back to you.

MAN: Your face will undergo involuntary changes. For example, you will blush . . .

WOMAN: There are many reasons for blushing. Sometimes, the very idea of being disbelieved produces embarassment . . .

MAN: Yes, but your eyes will falter. Your mouth also will indicate that what it speaks is false. If it is false . . . This is something I revere in you. I applaud the honesty of your features.

WOMAN: Yes, you applaud it because it gives you access to feelings which I prefer to guard. I cannot tell you how I loathe this in myself. I practise lying before mirrors.

MAN: To no avail.

WOMAN: As yet.

MAN: You will destroy the beauty of your character.

WOMAN: I cannot wait.

MAN: Why should you want secrets?

WOMAN: Because I do not want to be entered like a public place! (*She turns to him.*)
            I require my secrets. Inviolable avenues and little gardens, gated, fenced, and spiked my private — (*She issues a torrent.*)
            I have another lover — no I don't — I do — he adores me and I adore him — not really — but he gives me something — nothing much — this is nonsense — I am yours — yours only — beautiful man he —

no other man at all — preposterous — am I blushing — and now I feel guilt when I have nothing to be guilty of and if my lip trembles make of it what you want . . .! (*Pause. She begins to laugh.*)

Your face!

MAN: What of it? (*The* WOMAN *laughs, covering her mouth.*)

What of my face!

WOMAN: **Confusion and embarassment!** (*She stares.*)

You don't know what to . . . (*She turns her back quickly.*)

I cannot bear in a man.

I don't like that face, recover quickly, you look foolish, which I cannot bear in a man.

MAN: You dislike an expression which you yourself inspired —

WOMAN: **I cannot love a man with a face like that**. (*The* MAN *hangs his head.*)

I wish I'd not seen that . . . (*Pause*)

Obviously, this other man was necessary to me. (*The* MAN *drags a handkerchief from his pocket and drapes his face with it.*)

MAN: Please, stop torturing me . . . (*The* WOMAN *turns, looks at him.*)

Please . . . (*Pause. Then with deliberation.*)

WOMAN: He places one hand firmly on my arse . . . And with the other, draws up my skirt . . . in public sometimes, this . . .! In museums, or in restaurants . . . (*Pause. The* MAN *is still.*) And this hand is possessive, confident, and not polite . . . far from polite, it is — inspired and yet discreet . . . oh, so discreet he never pinches, pumps me, no, it is —

MAN: **Shut up**. (*Pause*)

WOMAN: And in his room, at the top of these stairs, dark stairs, he curses in his haste! And I am — flung, oh, toppled and — (*The* MAN *tears away the handkerchief. Instantly she covers her own face with her parasol.*)

MAN: Why do this to me . . .! (*Pause*)

WOMAN (*behind the parasol*): It isn't true. Inspired by some book, not true at all. I read too much. You always say it isn't good to read.

MAN: I'll kill you if it's true. (*Pause*)

Look at me.

WOMAN: No.

MAN: However foolish my expression, believe me I will kill you if it's —

WOMAN: **I don't know if it's true or not**. (*Pause*)

It's true that — what I just described — is what I wish.

MAN: Wish anything you like but is it —

WOMAN: I can't see your face so whether you are serious in your threat to kill me I can't be sure, and therefore whether what I said is fiction or confession is dependent now on pure intuition **yes I love him and he has my soul**! (*She lowers the parasol. Their eyes meet. Pause.*)

You were serious . . .! I can see it in your eyes! So serious, but I was lying.

MAN: You were not lying.

WOMAN: Was I not?

MAN: Not lying, no.

WOMAN: Teasing, rather.
MAN: Teasing, no.
WOMAN: My sense of humour governs me, you know. Why I have this humour, God knows, it protects me possibly from some terror I can't face, only with him am I not humorous . . .

The WOMAN AT THE MIRROR *looks up, over the rim. Her mouth hangs. The light shrinks until her face alone is illuminated. In the darkness, the passage of* THE DOUBLES, *at the terrible end of their struggle.*

SECOND DOUBLE: No . . . no . . . mercy . . .!
                      Mercy . . .!
                      Forgive . . .!
                      Forgive . . .!

A silence. The eyes of the WOMAN AT THE MIRROR *close. A dirty rain falls, staining her. She is a gargoyle. The light goes.*